Adult ESL Instruction
A Sourcebook

Lucy Madsen Guglielmino

LIFELONG LEARNING BOOKS
Teacher Resource Series
Scott, Foresman and Company
Glenview, Illinois • London

ISBN 0-673-24944-1

Library of Congress Cataloging-in-Publication Data

Guglielmino, Lucy Madsen.
    Adult ESL instruction : a sourcebook / Lucy Madsen Guglielmino.
        p.   cm. — (Teacher resource series)
    Includes bibliographical references.
    ISBN 0-673-24944-1
    1. English language—Study and teaching—Foreign speakers.
    2. Adult education.   I. Title.   II. Series.
PE1128.A2G78   1991
428'.007—dc20   90-40918
                                                                          CIP

Major portions of this publication were originally compiled and printed in 1984 through grant #AS4-06 to Florida Atlantic University from the Bureau of Adult/Community Education, Florida Department of Education, under the provisions of Section 310 of the Adult Education Act (Public Law 95-561). Comprehensive revisions and additions were made for this publication.

2 3 4 5 6 7–EBL–95 94 93 92

CONTENTS

PREFACE

Acronyms abound in the area of second-language learning. Three that may confuse a newcomer to the field are explained here.

EFL—English as a foreign language—refers to instruction in English for persons who do not intend to live in an English-speaking country. EFL classes might be taught in the student's native country (such as English classes in Europe for persons involved in international business), or they might be taught in this country (for example, the Summer Institute at Florida State University in Tallahassee for ARAMCO employees from Saudi Arabia).

ESL—English as a second language—applies to programs offered within an English-speaking country for persons who intend to remain there.

ESOL—English for speakers of other languages—is often used interchangeably with ESL. However, many use it as an umbrella term to cover both ESL and EFL instruction. In this book, however, the acronym ESL is used to refer to both English as a second language and English as a foreign language.

ESL places special demands on a teacher because ESL students—often feeling like strangers in a strange land—require far more than mere language instruction once or twice a week. They cannot leave their "foreign" language classroom to return to the safety and comfort of their native culture. Their physical and emotional well-being may depend on how quickly and how well they learn to communicate in English.

Given those special needs, this guide was written particularly with the ESL teacher in mind. Yet much of the discussion will be equally valuable to the EFL teacher or, for that matter, to any teacher of a foreign language.

Of paramount importance in preparing any kind of guide is the target population. What do teachers want? What did they need when they first started teaching? What kinds of things helped them? Hundreds of adult ESL and EFL teachers took the time to answer these questions, and their comments and suggestions were a strong factor in shaping this guide.

The guide grew out of and was initially funded by an Adult Education Act 310 Project. Thanks must first go to Mr. John Lawrence, Director of the Bureau for Adult and Community Education of the Florida Department of Eduation, who recognized the need for staff development for adult education ESL teachers and helped address that need by funding the project. Dr. Art Burrichter of Florida Atlantic University also provided invaluable support and encouragement.

Deep thanks must go as well to the project's statewide advisory committee, whose more than 200 years of collective language-teaching experience helped shape the project and the guide: Sheryl Beller, Helene Cusack, Rosa Diaz-Duque, Clifford Eberhardt, Bill Fanning, Alma Glover-Smith, Barbara Humak, Katharine Isbell, Dr. Jerry Messec, Anne Mock, Carolina McNaughton Nurik, and Faye Van Arsdall Schmelig. These individuals assisted with planning this guide, and some wrote vital sections. They were unfailingly generous with their time and information throughout the project. Others who provided valuable assistance are Lilliam Chisholm, Ruth Lieberman, and Sheila Smith. Caroline Bohlman's review comments helped shape the final manuscript.

Final thanks go to Paul, Joey, and Meg, who put up with me and supported my efforts.

Lucy Madsen Guglielmino

CHAPTER

1

Adult ESL: An Introduction

Lucy Madsen Guglielmino

THE TASK OF learning a new language as an adult is no small feat. Assisting a student to learn even enough English to survive requires a great deal of patience, empathy, and skill. The tremendous effort involved in running a successful adult ESL classroom is more than rewarded, however. Few students are more avidly interested in their subject matter than those who need to learn how to ask directions, those who cannot get a job because they cannot communicate, or those who must pass an English test to be admitted to a college or university in this country. This motivation and the bond that develops between student and teacher create an unusually warm and satisfying classroom situation.

WHO ARE ADULT ESL STUDENTS?

Who are the people who show up in ESL classrooms? What do they need and want? Adult ESL students usually come because each has an immediate need, yet those immediate needs and ultimate goals can vary widely.

One adult ESL student may speak a little English or none at all. Another may speak English very well but have limited abilities in reading and writing. Some ESL students are well-educated professionals in their countries; others are illiterate in their native language as well as in English. Some are interested in vocational training that involves specialized vocabulary; while the goal of others is to be able to read labels in a grocery store, find out where to catch the bus, or talk with their children's teachers.

ESL instruction is still in a period of emergence and refinement. From the many trends and approaches, however, one point has become increasingly clear: For students (and teacher) to succeed, ESL students must work with materials relevant to their most immediate language needs.

MEETING THEIR LANGUAGE NEEDS

Because of the diversity of students' needs as well as backgrounds and goals, a variety of ESL programs are offered. Some of the most common are explained below.

Survival ESL focuses on the skills needed for basic survival, such as asking for and understanding directions, handling money, and filling out simple forms.

ESL/Literacy emphasizes learning how to read and write English.

Pre-Vocational ESL teaches the skills and language necessary to get and keep a job, such as filling out a job application and being interviewed. Pre-vocational ESL covers work-related cultural attitudes as well.

Vocational ESL (VESL) is ESL related directly to vocational training. It is usually offered concurrently with the vocational training. In VESL the ESL teacher works closely with the vocational instructor to ensure timely introduction of appropriate vocabulary and grammar structures.

English for Special Purposes (ESP) refers to vocational ESL/EFL at a professional level. ESP serves students with strong academic abilities who need language skills related to fields such as engineering, business, or computer science.

TOEFL Preparation focuses on the vocabulary, listening comprehension, reading comprehension, and writing ability necessary to pass the Test of English as a Foreign Language (TOEFL), required for entry into most colleges and universities.

Academic Support ESL/EFL assists non-native students who are enrolled in academic programs.

ESL students come to these programs because they choose to, not because they have been coerced. But just as these adults voluntarily come, they will "vote with their feet" and disappear if they are not getting what they want. To give them what they want (and need), the teacher of ESL students must understand and accept them: first, as fellow human beings; second, as products of their cultures; and last, as adult learners with specific learning needs.

MEETING THEIR LEARNING NEEDS

Among the most urgent needs of adult ESL learners are the following:

1. *A teacher-student relationship based on mutual respect.* Adults expect to be treated like adults. They expect to have their experiences and opinions valued. There is often a temptation to treat ESL students like children, since their speech is childlike and they need a great deal of the kind of drill used with young children. An inappropriate classroom atmosphere results if that temptation is not avoided.

2. *Involvement in the classroom.* Student involvement is a good policy in any classroom, but it is especially important for adults in general and adult ESL students in particular. Students learn by doing. Probably the best single indication of the quality of an ESL classroom is the ratio of student speech or writing to teacher speech. The ESL student needs to *practice using English*, not hear someone else talk about English.

Students should be encouraged to share their experiences, questions, and cultural information. They are also more comfortable if they have some chance to voice their preferences: for topics to be covered, the order of the day's activities, or field-trip sites, for example. Lessons built around their activities and experiences are more meaningful and therefore are retained longer. Most important, they provide a valuable boost to students' self-esteem.

3. *Relevant instruction.* An ESL course must begin with a mutual process of identifying the gaps between where students are and where they need to be. The degree to which students can contribute to this process will vary with their language proficiency, but their input is important. The targeted level of English proficiency, the content of instruction, and its sequencing should be determined by their goals. The vocabulary, grammar structures, and dialogues they work with must have parallels in real life; they must be immediately applicable.

4. *A climate of teacher warmth and empathy.* Many adults feel uncomfortable in a classroom situation. Many have had unpleasant experiences in previous educational settings. Regardless of their memories of school, adult ESL students usually feel quite uncomfortable because they cannot use English as well as they would like (if at all). Teacher warmth, acceptance, and empathy are particularly important to them. A large body of research shows that if a teacher is warm, caring, and enthusiastic, students learn more.

To create a positive and accepting climate in your classroom—

- Smile.

- Remember names.

- Greet students as they enter and wish them well as they leave.

- Notice and freely praise their successes.

- Choose your words carefully when responding to errors. For example, avoid such negative remarks as, "No," "That's not right," and "That's wrong." Instead, say, "Let's try that again" or simply, "Once again," and repeat the phrase or question. Such actions may seem minor, but the smallest things, repeated often, can create a large impact.

5. *Opportunities for problem-solving and self-directed learning.* Such skill building is a must for any adult program. It is easier at the higher levels of ESL instruction, but should be incorporated wherever possible. For example, students can be asked to describe what they would do in everyday problem situations, such as returning something to a store or asking for a day off to attend a wedding. Their input can be used to build practice dialogues. In addition, if you can let students *find* an answer rather than just feeding it to them, they begin to develop skills that will help them the rest of their lives. This self-directed learning helps reduce the possibility that they will become too dependent on you and hinder their own development. The old Chinese philosophy is as true today as it was centuries ago:

> Give a man a fish,
>   and he eats for a day;
> Teach a man to fish,
>   and he eats for a lifetime.

6. *Opportunities for success.* Adult ESL students have their egos battered every day. They are often looked down upon or treated rudely because many people in our culture equate "different" with "wrong" or mistakenly associate the lack of ability to communicate in English with a lack of intelligence. As a result of these attitudes and their own feelings of communicative inadequacy, ESL students often experience a great deal of frustration. They need opportunities to succeed and to be recognized for that success every day.

One way to provide such opportunities is to encourage students to set small daily or weekly goals. As the goals are achieved, the students can be congratulated and congratulate themselves on their progress. If they face only that major goal, "to learn English" every day, it begins to seem impossible to achieve. The satisfaction of achieving smaller goals provides the motivation and encouragement to continue.

Opportunities for success can be maximized in almost every type of classroom activity. Careful planning is especially important in oral drills, where students must perform before the group. When practicing a dialogue, for example, have the whole group respond first. Then divide the class in half and have each half respond. Next have students volunteer to respond, and finally call on each person. In this way, each student has a better chance of mastering the language before being asked to perform individually.

7. *A comfortable yet stimulating environment.* A classroom can be an uncomfortable physical environment, with small, hard seats and extremes of heat or cold. Many adults may have already put in a full day's work before they get to class; they will be tired. Anything that can be done to increase their comfort and liven up the class—varying teaching methods, using audiovisual aids, changing the pace of activities—will help students concentrate.

8. *Cultural orientation.* Effective communication depends on many other things besides vocabulary, structures, and pronunciation. A person who will not look into a job interviewer's eyes will probably not be hired. A new employee who is consistently late for work is likely to lose the job. Yet these behaviors, which seem so strange to us, are perfectly acceptable in other cultures. In Asian cultures, looking directly at a person in a position of authority is considered an insult. In Latin cultures, being on time does not carry the importance attached to it in this country.

Culture involves a wide variety of things that we tend to take for granted: values, attitudes, goals, gestures, courtesies, eye contact, spatial awareness, time awareness, modes of dress, habits of cleanliness, and much more. If an ESL student acts in a strange or an annoying way, the behavior is probably a part of the student's native culture. Understanding cultural differences helps both teacher and students deal with them more effectively.

A corollary need of some ESL students is teacher sensitivity to culture shock. Remember Alvin Toffler's best-seller, *Future Shock*? He described the negative impact that rapid change can have on an individual within the *same* culture. Imagine how easily a person who is trying to fit into a totally *new* culture may become disoriented, discouraged, depressed, and exhausted from trying to cope. ESL teachers must be attuned to this possibility in their classrooms, especially among students who are political refugees.

THE ESL TEACHER AS LIFELINE

Adult ESL teachers are a hard-working and dedicated group. Most are driven by a strong desire to find out what works for their students. Why? Because their students need so much. When other adults look to you as the key to being able to function fully in this society, when they are willing to put in long hours after working full-time jobs, when they light up at understanding a new word or structure, when they respond so intensely to a few words of praise, a deep teacher-student bond develops. In essence, you are their lifeline—their key to survival and success.

This rich relationship should be enjoyed, welcomed, even nurtured—but it should also be kept in perspective. Early in the language-learning process, students must be able to feel that they have found someone they can rely on to help them in this strange new language and culture, but *help* is the key word. From the very beginning, students should use English as much as possible and be involved in activities that build their confidence and self-reliance. Whenever possible, the students, not the teacher, should be the focus of the classroom. It is gratifying to be the guru, the center of knowledge, and yes, perhaps even the star—but it is much more rewarding to make students the stars and watch them grow more confident in their language abilities. The purpose of a lifeline, after all, is to get the struggler to the boat.

The remainder of this guide offers specific suggestions and resources on how to be such a lifeline—on how to meet the language needs and the learning needs of ESL students.

2

Cultural Considerations in Teaching ESL

Julia A. Spinthourakis

WOULD YOU THINK twice about sitting with your legs crossed and the sole of your shoe facing your listener? You would if you were a native speaker of Arabic. People who speak different languages view the world differently, said Edward Sapir in 1929. To lay an important cornerstone in mastering another language, an ESL teacher must help students recognize and understand the cultural aspects of that language.

Students come to an ESL classroom with a lot of "cultural baggage." Cultural baggage in this instance should not be viewed negatively, but neither should its impact be underestimated. It is a formidable element that impinges on everything a student does and feels.

Language and culture are said to be inseparable. To attempt to teach students a new language without first understanding their culture and seeing where your own is at counterpoint to it can lead to missed or misunderstood messages. The end result is confusion and frustration, if not outright anger. Effective ESL teachers are keenly aware of the cultural differences and similarities between the American reality in which they live and the one each student is bringing to their classrooms.

This is not to say that you must become an authority on the nuances of all the diverse cultures that may turn up in your class. While that goal may be admirable, it is one that the teacher who has eighteen different language backgrounds in a single classroom is unlikely to reach. Two tasks, however, are set before you: Strive to (a) be sensitive to differences in behaviors, attitudes, and values that students may exhibit and (b) become aware of the behaviors, attitudes, and values that distinguish your own culture, your own reality.

If, for example, you know that you will have a class made up of one or more distinct cultural groups, it makes sense to learn as much as you can about the unique cultural characteristics of those groups. If time doesn't allow for such planning, don't despair; just tread softly. Note how your students behave. Then turn to the second task, knowing what distinguishes your own culture, and use it as the basis of your ESL lessons. Ask your students how some aspect of culture compares with their own, and they will let you know — verbally, figuratively, and/or behaviorally.

The key is to be observant as well as knowledgeable. Your observations of students' reactions to the language and cultural information you give them will allow you to identify cultural views that contrast with your own. They will also help you recognize how these contrasting views color the way your students relate to their present reality.

EXAMINING CULTURAL BEHAVIORS

An ESL teacher needs to be conscious of cultural behaviors that we take for granted, things that we do automatically without question. Take, for example, how we read. We begin at the top left of a page, proceed to the right and move back to the left until the page is complete. "So?" you may say. Readers of Arabic and Hebrew begin at the right and from what we consider the back of the book. They also write in this manner. Think about what this cultural trait means in terms of a writing lesson or even a transcription lesson.

Americans tend to be in a hurry, are regarded as being extremely informal, and appear to be little concerned about social distinctions. We also are highly competitive on an individual basis. All these national traits or attitudes are important parts of a teacher's own cultural baggage. Each can become the basis of a language lesson.

Other aspects of everyday life that differ among cultures and can form part of ESL lessons are —

1. family structures

2. the buyer-seller relationship

3. humor

4. politics

5. advertising and the media

6. eating habits

7. risk taking

8. acceptable social behavior

9. traditional social values

10. time

Another aspect of culture and therefore of language that needs to be addressed is the taboo—especially the verbal taboo. A verbal taboo is language that is not tolerated—either in the new culture or in the student's native culture. As an ESL teacher, you must often find a way to show students that what is acceptable to say in their culture is not acceptable here, and that what may be unacceptable in their culture is perfectly acceptable here.

Your awareness, then, needs to extend to the cultural codes that govern social interaction. Codes identify what may be discussed, how it may be discussed, and what extra-lingual actions are appropriate. Think for a moment. Native speakers and listeners don't need to exchange a lot of information verbally because they are able to use and interpret unspoken codes. If you see someone with arms crossed, for example, do you get the sense that the person is really open to a conversation (given, of course, that he or she is not merely cold and trying to warm up)? On the other hand, you wouldn't think twice about sitting with your legs crossed and the sole of your shoe facing your listener. Yet in Muslim cultures, that physical position would send a message of outrage.

Consider, too, the amount of space you allow between yourself and a partner in conversation. You mentally "rope off" a certain amount of space. If that space is entered, you probably move back a step. Americans like to keep a few feet between themselves, except in very intimate situations. That preference is not found in all cultures. For Greeks, the amount of space between speaker and listener is radically reduced. Therefore, if a Greek student learning English is not aware of this difference and intrudes into an American's space, the verbal message he or she is giving will become garbled. The American will be trying to decode the verbal message while simultaneously receiving a cultural message at counterpoint to that intended. The result is a form of dissonance, static, or noise—a jamming of the message, if you will.

Cultural codes include gestures, facial expression, physical position, proximity, tactile behavior, areas of silence, and time. Not understanding the relevance of these culturally determined codes can often lead to unintended messages being sent or received. A great deal has been written on these codes. Some books that you may want to examine for further information are listed at the end of this chapter.

RESOURCES FOR CULTURAL AWARENESS

To incorporate awareness of these cultural codes in your language instruction, structure your lessons as much as possible around real uses of language. Look beyond textbooks for additional teaching materials.

Activities that involve experiences in real-life contexts are one way to instill cultural awareness. Field trips are very good, as is role play. Use realia and concrete situations that students are likely to be confronted with in everyday life.

Cartoons, both cinematic and print, newspaper advice columns like "Ann Landers," "Dear Abby," and "Miss Manners," and magazine ads are materials where cultural information can be found. Television commercials and daytime soap operas can also be used (with a caveat to students that not everyone in the country lives as the celluloid people do). With that qualification, TV shows can be an excellent way to teach language related to emotions, relationships, and chronology. Paperbacks that chronicle generations of families are also available, as are videos that have been specifically tailored to the language and cultural learning needs of ESL students. Consider also using proverbs in the students' native languages with their counterparts in English.

The list of available resource material is seemingly endless. The key is to look around you and identify what your students bring with them as well as what they need to know in order to function in society. Once you've amassed a list, see how you can use it as the content of lessons, lessons that include all the skills students must master to survive and succeed in their new reality.

All language takes place within the framework of culture and social settings. Whether language is verbal or written, someone will receive it and decipher it according to a cultural context. Therefore, as an adult ESL teacher, you need to ensure that your teaching of language includes the cultural awareness students must have to communicate appropriately in their new cultural context.

Bibliography

Hall, E. T. 1978. *Beyond culture.* Garden City, N.Y.: Doubleday.

Hall, E. T. 1959. *The silent language.* New York: Fawcett.

Morain, G. C. 1978. *Kinesics and cross-cultural understanding.* Arlington, Va.: Center for Applied Linguistics.

Sapir, E. 1929. The status of linguistics as a science. *Language* 5: 205–214.

Seelye, H. N. 1981. *Teaching culture.* Skokie, Ill.: National Textbook Company.

C H A P T E R
3

A Brief History
of ESL Teaching

John F. Haskell and Jerry L. Messec

IT HAS BEEN said that those who refuse to study history are condemned to repeat it. Others contend that all history, even that of language teaching (Stevick 1971), is cyclical and that we should study it to learn where we are going. In any case, a bit of historical perspective on ESL teaching in the United States should prove to be valuable. Such a review will help you pinpoint the approaches of various textbooks you have available. Also, since the method in adult ESL instruction is "Use whatever works, for those specific students in that particular class," you may gain from this overview some ideas to incorporate in your own eclectic approach.

ESL teaching in the United States generally has been viewed as part of the broader field of foreign language teaching, and for a long time its development paralleled that of the teaching of German, French, Spanish, and other languages. It is true that ESL instruction has been subject to some of the same historical influences and has passed through the same periods of change. Yet the special needs of ESL teaching have always set it apart from foreign language teaching per se. Those special needs are generally highlighted by ESL students' immediate need to use the language. Most adult ESL students are not pursuing literary interests. They are not preparing for a visit to another country. They are not studying a new language for the prestige or intellectual challenge (at least not primarily). Most adult ESL students are learning English because they must. They need to be able to use English, some kind of English, as quickly as possible. They are involved in language learning in a way that foreign-language students in the United States or EFL students in non-English speaking countries are not.

The argument in the 1950s and 1960s over whether teachers of English to speakers of other languages were *second* language or *foreign* language teachers has, in large part, been resolved. We now have a greater understanding of the different needs of the EFL and the ESL student (Maple 1987). An understanding of the different environments in which these students learn English and of the different goals they have in learning English is more and more reflected in the textbooks available to the teacher (Flamm, Northam, and Yorkey 1990; Maple 1988–9).

GRAMMAR-TRANSLATION METHOD

Most foreign-language teaching in the United States has been (and possibly still is) conducted basically as a study of how the grammar of the target language works, through reading (literature) and translation. Instruction is generally in English, even though the student is trying to learn Spanish or French or German. Use of the target language outside the classroom is negligible, if available at all, and any hope of ever using the language in real life rests generally far in the future. This method, used in much of foreign language and EFL teaching and until the 1950s a much-used approach in ESL teaching, is called the grammar-translation method.

With the grammar-translation method, the purpose of instruction is primarily to develop competence in reading and writing. The grammar-translation approach views language as a system of rules to be taught and tested, and teaching is generally done in the students' first language rather than in the target language. The expectation is that few will ever use the target language at all.

Both the teacher and students assume that by studying the grammar rules of the new language and adding vocabulary and some application work, such as translation and the conjugation of verbs, the new language will be learned. The well-documented lack of success of this assumption for all but a few students has not changed the opinion of most teachers and students. The grammar-translation method still holds a high position of academic respectability in this country and abroad—a respectability ultimately derived from the prestige of Latin studies and based on the idea that grammar study encourages clear thinking, the tradition of a well-rounded education, and the sanctity of literature and academic translation. Even the abject failure of generation after generation of foreign-language students has not dissuaded many.

While those studying foreign languages in the United States might accept, even expect, failure to master a foreign language, ESL students cannot afford such lack of success. ESL teachers expect more direct results in their work and long ago began to try other methods.

THE DIRECT METHOD AND
THE ORAL APPROACH

At the end of the nineteenth century and for the first half of the twentieth century, one of the most promising alternatives to grammar-translation was the direct method, which stressed spoken language and the use of the target language as the medium of instruction from the beginning. Francois Gouin (Gouin 1880) and M. D. Berlitz (Berlitz 1887) promoted direct method approaches at the end of the nineteenth century as more "natural" methods of learning, since they emphasized speaking first and utilized more natural language-learning techniques, such as the sequenced presentation of real language and the inductive learning of grammar. Carl Kraus brought the direct method to the United States in the early part of the twentieth century (Kraus 1916) and in 1929 Emile deSauze (deSauze 1929) brought his version of the direct method (especially for the teaching of French) to this country. The Danish scholar Otto Jesperson and Harold E. Palmer in England developed more scientific versions of the direct method, sometimes called the oral approach (Jesperson 1904; Palmer 1921). The oral approach, with its systematic and graded presentation of language, restricted vocabulary, and, like the direct method, inductive presentation of grammar, was the approach used by the British well into the 1960s (West 1960; Hornby 1961).

THE AUDIOLINGUAL METHOD
AND ITS OFFSPRING

During World War II the need arose for "instant" speakers of languages for countries into which GI's were being sent. This need helped bring together concepts from the fields of psychology and linguistics, as well as ideas from the direct method and the oral approach, into a new language-teaching pedagogy. From behavioral psychology this pedagogy took such ideas as stimulus-response and positive reinforcement along with the notion of the brain as a tabula rasa, or clean slate, ready for input. From the new science of descriptive linguistics, it adopted the structural nature of language, with its systems of phonology (sounds), morphology (word formation), and syntax (grammar). From the direct method it borrowed the practice of teaching language in the target language, with its emphasis on the more natural order of speaking before reading and writing and the inductive presentation of grammar. And from the oral approach it took the notions of pattern practice, mimicry and memorization, and vocabulary control. This new language-teaching pedagogy was called the audiolingual method (ALM).

With the audiolingual method the goal is spoken language. Rules and vocabulary are taught in the context of everyday life. This approach emphasizes oral skills and delays reading and writing. It views language learning as training through practice. Dialogue memorization and pattern practice (structural drills) are typical teaching techniques. The ALM also emphasizes the teaching of grammar sequentially and inductively, the use of the target language in teaching from the very beginning, the immediate correction of error, the control of vocabulary and context, and the insistence on teaching one item at a time, not moving on until the new item has been learned. The ALM gained much favor in the United States as a second-language teaching method in the 1950s and 1960s. Its practical approach to language seemed especially appropriate for ESL teaching. In fact, it soon became the standard method for those who were formally trained in ESL instruction (Fries 1945; Lado 1964; Finocchiaro 1965).

The Offspring

However, the traditional ALM approach did not coincide for long with what experienced ESL teachers found to be practical or workable in the classroom. ALM programs generally compartmentalize content into such separate classes as pronunciation, grammar, conversation, reading, and composition; they seldom provide an opportunity for the integration of all the areas being taught. The 1960s and 1970s, therefore, saw the introduction of such modified audiolingual methods as the Situational Reinforcement of Eugene Hall (Hall 1978), the Silent Way of Caleb Gattegno (Gattegno 1976), James Asher's Total Physical Response (Asher 1954), Georgi Lozanov's Suggestopedia (Lozanov 1971, 1978), and Father Charles Curran's Counseling-Learning (Curran 1976).

The 1960s and 1970s also saw such specialized program approaches as English for Academic Purposes (EAP), English for Special Purposes

(ESP), English for Science and Technology (EST), and Vocational English as a Second Language (VESL). Generally found in colleges and universities, EAP prepares students to enter fully into education in English (Jordan 1989). ESP is most commonly reflected in the EST programs instituted by the British in the oil-producing countries of the Middle East. ESP and EST are also found in such special training programs as those at Lackland Air Force Base in Texas for non-U.S. military personnel (Richards 1976). VESL programs are often found in the United States in junior and community colleges, generally in short-term programs that teach students both English and special job skills (Day 1982).

Each method, each program, attempted to correct or counter some perceived weakness in the more traditional ALM approach. Each of these attempts to modify or replace ALM brought to the classroom new ideas about how students learn language and how to meet their needs.

Situational Reinforcement, for example, stressed the importance—especially for adult students—of associating language with behavior by replacing the controlled, sterile, often nonsensical dialogues of the early ALM texts with real-life situations. These contexts reflected the real needs of adult students.

The Silent Way approach had the student take responsibility for learning, committing to the process rather than relying solely on the teacher for all direction and all input. The Silent Way also introduced a student to the "feel" of a language, any language, by stressing the importance of being comfortable with its sounds, its rhythm, and its intonation patterns.

Counseling-Learning stressed the importance of letting the students' needs and experiences direct the course of language acquisition. The role of the teacher was to act as an effective resource to student-centered needs—and as an equal participant in the learning process.

Suggestopedia emphasized the atmosphere in which students are taught, including the importance of positive thinking, reducing student anxiety, and subliminal learning (Hammerman 1979).

Asher's Total Physical Response system (TPR) emphasized the physical nature of the language act, the importance of multiple stimulus learning, and the active participation of the student.

None of these methods has been completely successful nor recognized, at least for long, as *the* method. The reason is not only their own limitations as solutions to the question of how we learn language but also in some part the commercialization of the training and materials that had to accompany many of them. Their inability to be accepted in teacher training institutions as singular methods of teaching ESL reflected the increasingly eclectic nature of language-teaching philosophy. Like the more traditional ALM and even, for a few, the grammar-translation method before it, each method worked for some; yet no method worked for everyone, teacher or student.

New Research, New Views

Despite the failure of each ALM offspring as *the* method, they all offered unique insights into language learning. In addition, the dominance of cognitive psychology and humanistic research in the 1960s, together with the increased interest in the nature of second-language acquisition and classroom-centered research of the 1970s, resulted in new and expanded views of language teaching and language learning.

The 1970s were also a period of political conflict between those who believed in the teaching of limited English proficient students in ESL programs versus those who favored bilingual/bicultural education. This conflict had a profound influence on classroom practices, as it challenged ESL teachers to move more rapidly toward a philosophy of teaching that was student-centered as opposed to method-centered. This student-centered philosophy revolved around an understanding of the various cultures of the new American, as well as American culture (Hall 1957; Buckingham 1981; Valdes 1986). It fostered the recognition of the experience and linguistic knowledge that the ESL student brings to the language classroom. It forced educators to move from a philosophy of the teaching of language and culture as a replacive act to one viewing it as an additive process.

In 1967 S. Pit Corder introduced the notion of systematic error as opposed to random error and set the stage for much of the language research of the 1970s. For example, research by Larry Selinker (1974) and Marina Burt (1975) showed that ESL student errors were more often caused by such things as fossilization, poor teaching or learning strategies, and overgeneralization rather than interference from the student's first language. Gardner and Lambert (1972) studied motivation in the classroom, suggesting both integrative and instrumental factors. Widdowson (1983) and Wilkins (1976) directed ESL teachers toward English for Special Purposes programs and notional-functional syllabuses. Oller and Richards (1973), Krashen (1982), and Smith (1983) pushed the field toward more natural, pragmatic approaches to language teaching. Ruth Crymes (1980) explained the different strategies learners use, David Eskey (1976) praised the discovery of teachers and learners as human beings, and Earl Stevick (1981), interviewing successful language learners, discovered once again that we all learn differently, that natural language learning is to some extent based on the learner's view of learning, and that it is often these attitudes and expectations, different for each of us, that affect our success.

COMMUNICATIVE COMPETENCE

The audiolingual method, born from World War II military foreign-language teaching successes and modified in the 1960s by the intuitive discoveries of various methodologists, was transformed by the sociolinguistic theories and research of the 1970s (Strevens 1977; Widdowson 1978) into a more communicative approach to ESL teaching. Dell Hymes (1972), Christina Bratt Paulston (1974), and Sandra Savignon (1976) presented the notion of communicative competence as a goal of the classroom.

The communicative approach is based on a view of language as a system of human communication. Sometimes it consciously teaches rules, sometimes not. All learning is done in context, and the context must be appropriate for the learner. Derived from the ALM, the communicative approach often uses the same techniques but adds communicative, meaningful activities such as role plays, problem solving, and small group interaction and emphasizes communicative competence — the sociolinguistic notion of language use (function) in addition to usage (form). Canale and Swain (1980) defined communicative competence as linguistic competence (language usage), sociolinguistic competence (language use), discourse competence (coherence and cohesion), and strategic competence (communication repair strategies).

The communicative approaches of the late 1970s and early 1980s led ESL teaching away from a strictly linguistic emphasis and toward more natural, pragmatic, and functional uses of language. This has proved a rich field for the development of language studies and has resulted in the creation of a range of new classroom techniques in the 1980s. Research gave ESL teachers practical information both for discussing the progress and problems of learners and for planning coherent teaching programs that include both language rules and language performance (Richards 1984). It also provided a new set of methods, bandwagons, and gurus (Clarke 1982, 1984) such as the pragmatic approach (Oller and Richard-Amato 1983), the "new" natural approach (Krashen and Terrell 1982), the integrated approach (Blair 1982), proficiency oriented instruction (Omaggio 1986), the comprehension approach (Winitz 1981), and the teacher training theory of FOCUS (Fanselow 1987).

THE "NEW" NATURAL APPROACH

The new natural method — similar to its precursor in name, the natural methodology of the direct method period — is one of the many newer modifications of the ALM. Much as Gouin, Gattegno, and Curran discovered their methods through their own language learning experiences, the natural method also began as the intuitive idea of how language was learned. Its underlying hypotheses were the catchwords of the 1980s. The analysis and criticism of these hypotheses fed the discussion and research that made the eclecticism of the 1980s even more effective and resulted, perhaps, in a natural method progeny (McLaughlin 1978; Higgs and Clifford 1982).

The natural approach supports two often conflicting events in language classrooms: conscious rule learning and unconscious language acquisition. It is concerned with language as human communication and is adaptable to a broad range of language teaching methods and techniques. This "new" natural approach emphasizes the importance of listening activities at the beginning of instruction; real, pragmatic, and functional activities for language acquisition; the integrative nature of language learning; the naturalness and value of making errors; the appropriate use of language; the importance of motivation; and a recognition of such hypotheses as the natural order of acquisition, affective filter, fossilization and feedback, language monitoring, language acquisition (versus learning), and comprehensible input.

ECLECTICISM

Near the end of the 1970s Haskell (1978) asked if there was in fact an eclectic method and listed several items that reflected the eclecticism of language teaching. An eclectic method is one that utilizes the best, most appropriate, and/or most useful parts of existing methods—a principled versus an irrational eclecticism. There is the danger in eclecticism, of course, of putting various selected raw materials together and creating a Frankenstein monster. The use of the term *eclectic method* also suggests, in one sense, a single, best method—almost the antithesis of eclecticism.

Eclecticism is not a method, then, but an approach or philosophy of teaching—the selection and use of appropriate techniques for ESL. Generally communicative in nature, it reflects what is understood from second-language research. However, while trends in second-language research would emphasize natural, pragmatic, and integrated language learning, *no* technique is eliminated if it supports the purpose of the student's language study (though such tactics as constant and immediate error correction, mechanical drills, and formal testing are felt to be in opposition to natural learning strategies). A clear evaluation and understanding of what techniques actually accomplish is emphasized (as opposed to using them just because they are familiar and comfortable).

In some ways, ESL teachers are listening more and more to people outside the general field of language teaching (Haskell 1988), and they are rediscovering techniques that the oral and audiolingual methodologists such as Palmer, West, and Charles C. Fries espoused (Ellis 1988). The close scrutiny and eventual acceptance of such ideas as the cloze procedure (Oller 1973; Haskell 1973), the language experience approach (Rigg 1977), and the need to teach listening skills (Morley 1972) reflect not only teachers' willingness to accept new and carefully evaluated ideas (Gaies 1986) but also their classroom eclecticism. Their philosophy of teaching based on the needs of students, their knowledge of language learning, and their capabilities as teachers (Judd 1983; Auerbach and Burgess 1985) are also evident.

If ESL teachers have learned anything in the trek from grammar-translation to eclectic or integrative language teaching, it is that each cycle, each leap forward, each bandwagon, while not providing a learning model suitable for everyone, reflects both questions about and new understandings of language learning and language teaching. ESL teachers must listen to and evaluate each new idea in terms of their students' needs and take what they can use in light of their own capabilities (Brown 1980a; Chaudron 1988; Beebe 1988).

Thanks to Elliot Judd of the University of Illinois–Chicago, Barbara Speicher of DePaul University of Chicago, and Cathy Day of Eastern Michigan University for their time and interest in reading and reviewing this chapter.

Bibliography

Asher, 1954. *Learning another language through action.* Los Gatos, Calif.: Sky Oak Productions.

Auerbach, E., and Burgess, 1985. The hidden curriculum of survival ESL. *TESOL Quarterly,* 19:4.

Bartley, D. 1979. *The adult basic education handbook.* New York: Collier Macmillan.

Beebe, L., ed. 1988. *Issues in second language acquisition: Multiple perspectives.* New York: Newbury House.

Berlitz, M. D. 1887. *Methode Berlitz.* New York: Berlitz and Company.

Blair, R. 1982. *Innovative approaches to language teaching.* Rowley, Mass.: Newbury House.

Brown, H. 1980a. Revised edition, 1987. *Principles of language learning and teaching.* Englewood Cliffs, N.J.: Prentice-Hall.

– – –. 1980b. The role of teacher feedback in preventing the fossilized errors of second language learners. *Ontario TESOL Newsletter.*

Buckingham, T. 1981. Four dimensions of intercultural communications. In *Teaching ESL: A pre-methods text,* J. Haskell and T. Buckingham. Working draft.

Burt, M. 1975. Error correction in the adult ESL classroom. *TESOL Quarterly,* 9:1.

Canale, M., and Swain, M. 1980. Theoretical bases of communicative approaches to second language teaching and testing. *Applied Linguistics,* 1.

Chaudron, C. 1988. Classroom research: Recent research and findings. In *AILA Review,* 5, 1988, ed. Gabriele Kasper, Amsterdam: Free University Press.

Clarke, M. 1982. On bandwagons, tyranny and common sense. *TESOL Quarterly,* 16:4.

— — —. 1984. On the nature of technique: What do we owe the gurus? *TESOL Quarterly,* 18:4.

Crymes, R. 1980. Current trends in ESL instruction. *TESOL Newsletter,* 14:4. Paper presented at Indiana TESOL, October 1980. Also in *Selected articles from the TESOL newsletter: 1966–1983,* ed. J. Haskell. Washington, D.C.: TESOL.

Curran, C. 1976. *Counseling-learning in second languages.* Apple River, Ill.: Apple River Press.

Day, E. 1982. Going beyond career education. *TESOL Newsletter,* 16:4. Also in *Selected articles from the TESOL Newsletter: 1966–1983.* ed. J. Haskell. Washington, D.C.: TESOL.

DeSauze, E. 1929. *The Cleveland plan for teaching modern languages.* Philadelphia: Winston.

Diller, K. 1978. *The language teaching controversy.* Rowley, Mass.: Newbury House.

Ellis, R. 1988. The role of practice in classroom language learning. In *AILA Review,* 5, 1988, ed. Gabriele Kasper, Amsterdam: Free University Press.

Eskey, D. 1976. A revolutionary new idea: The student and teacher as human beings. *Language Learning,* 26, 1.

Fanselow, J. 1987. *Breaking rules.* New York: Longman.

Finocchiarro, M. 1965. *English as a second language: From theory to practice.* New York: Regents.

Flamm, J.; Northram, L.; and Yorkey, R. 1990. *The English advantage.* New York: Newbury House.

Fries, C. 1945. *Teaching and learning English as a foreign language.* Ann Arbor: University of Michigan Press.

Gaies, S. 1986. Research in TESOL: Romance, precision and reality. Speech given at Sixth Annual Midwest TESOL Conference, Ann Arbor, Michigan, November 8, 1986. *TESOL Newsletter,* 21:2.

Gardner, R., and Lambert, W. 1972. *Attitudes and motivation in second language learning.* Rowley, Mass.: Newbury House.

Gattegno, C. 1976. *The common sense of teaching foreign languages.* New York: Educational Solutions.

Gouin, F. 1880. Translated by H. Swan and Y. Betis. 1892. *The art of teaching and studying languages.* London: George Philip Co.

Hall, E. J. 1978. Situational reinforcement. *TESOL Newsletter,* 12:2. From *Situational reinforcement, nucleus course in English* 1968–9. Washington, D.C.: Institute of Modern Languages.

Hall, E. T. 1957. *The silent language.* Garden City, N.Y.: Doubleday.

Hammerman, M. 1979. Suggestion and education. *TESOL Newsletter,* 13:4. Also in *Selected articles from the TESOL Newsletter: 1966–1963,* ed. J. Haskell. Washington, D.C.: TESOL. See also *Commonalities of self-directed learning and learning in self-help groups.* Doctoral dissertation, Northern Illinois University, 3 May, 1989.

Haskell, J. 1973. Refining the cloze procedure for ESL. *English Record,* 25:4.

––– 1978. An eclectic method? *TESOL Newsletter,* 12:2. Also in *Selected articles from the TESOL newsletter: 1966-1983,* ed. J. Haskell. Washington, D.C.: TESOL, 1986.

––– 1988. What I've learned from the gurus. Plenary speech given at the 22nd Annual TESOL Convention, Chicago, Ill., March 11, 1988.

Higgs, T., and Clifford, R. 1982. The push towards communication. In *Curriculum, Competence, and the Foreign Language Teacher,* ed. T. V. Higgs, ACTFL Foreign Language Education Series, vol. 13. Lincolnwood, Ill.: National Textbook Company.

Hornby, A. 1961. *The teaching of structural words and selective patterns.* London: Oxford Press.

Howatt, A. P. R. 1984. *A history of English language teaching.* Oxford: Oxford University Press.

Hymes, D. 1972. On communicative competence. In *Sociolinguistics,* ed. J. B. Pride and J. Holmes, Harmondsworth: Penguin Books.

Ilyin, D., and Tragardth, T. 1978. *Classroom practices in adult ESL.* Washington, D.C.: TESOL.

Jesperson, O. 1904. Reprinted in 1940. *How to teach a foreign language.* London: Longman.

Jordan, R. R. 1989. English for academic purposes: state of the art. In *Language teaching: International abstracting journal for language teachers and applied linguists.* London: Cambridge Press.

Judd, E. 1983. TESOL as a political act: A moral question. In *On TESOL 83: The question of control,* ed. J. Handscombe, R. Orem, and B. Taylor, Washington, D.C.: TESOL, 1984.

Krashen, S. 1982. *Principles and practice in second language acquisition.* Oxford: Pergamon Press.

Krashen, S., and Terrell, T. 1983. *The natural approach: Language acquisition in the classroom.* Haywood, Calif.: Alemany Press.

Kraus, C. 1916. *The direct method in modern languages.* New York: Charles Scribner.

Lado, R. 1957. *Linguistics across cultures.* Ann Arbor: University of Michigan Press.

——— 1964. *Language teaching: A scientific approach.* New York: McGraw-Hill.

Larsen-Freeman, D. 1986. *Techniques and principles in language teaching.* New York: Oxford University Press.

Littlewood, W. 1981. *Communicative language teaching.* Cambridge: Cambridge University Press.

Lozanov, G. 1978. Orig. 1971. *Suggestology and outlines of suggestopedy.* New York: Gordon and Breach.

Maple, R. 1987. TESL versus TEFL: What's the difference? *TESOL Newsletter,* 21:2. (See also updated ms. 1987.)

——— 1988–9. *New Wave: American English course for EFL.* London: Longman.

McLaughlin, B. 1978. The monitor model: Some methodological considerations *Language Learning,* 28.

Morley, J. 1972. *Improving aural comprehension.* Ann Arbor: University of Michigan Press.

——— 1987. Current directions on teaching English to speakers of other languages: A state of the art synopsis. *TESOL Newsletter,* 21:2.

Oller, J. 1973. Cloze tests of second language proficiency in ESL and what they mean. *Language Learning,* 25:3.

Oller, J., and Richards, J. 1973. *Focus on the learner: Pragmatic perspectives for the language teacher.* Rowley, Mass.: Newbury House.

Oller, J., and Richard-Amato, P. 1983. *Methods that work: A smorgasbord of ideas for language teachers.* Rowley, Mass.: Newbury House.

Omaggio, A. 1986. *Teaching language in context: Proficiency oriented instruction.* Boston, Mass.: Heinle and Heinle.

Palmer, H. 1917. *The scientific study and teaching of languages.* London: Harrap. Reissued 1968. London: Oxford University Press.

———. 1921. *The oral method of teaching languages.* Cambridge: W. Heffer and Sons.

Paulston, C. 1974. Linguistic and communicative competence. *TESOL Quarterly,* 18:4.

Richards, J. 1976. *Teaching English for science and technology.* Singapore: SEAMO Regional English Language Centre.

Richards, J. 1984. The secret life of methods. *TESOL Quarterly,* 18:1.

Richards, J., and Rodgers, T. 1986. *Approaches and methods in language teaching: A description and analysis.* Cambridge: Cambridge University Press.

Rigg, P. 1977. Beginning to read the LEA Way. *SPEAQ Journal*, Autumn.

Savignon, S. 1976. Communicative competence: Theory and classroom practice. Keynote address, Cultural States Conference on Teaching Foreign Languages. Detroit, Michigan, April 23, 1976. See also *Communicative competence: Theory and practice.* Reading, Mass.: Addison-Wesley, 1983.

Selinker, L. 1974. Interlanguage. In *New frontiers in second language learning,* ed. J. Schumann and N. Stenson, Rowley, Mass.: Newbury House.

Smith, F. 1983. The promise and threat of microcomputers for language learning. In *On TESOL 83: The question of control,* ed. J. Handscombe, R. Orem, and B. Taylor. Washington, D.C.: TESOL, 1984.

Stern, H. H. 1983. *Fundamental concepts of language teaching.* Oxford: Oxford University Press.

Stevick, E. 1971. *Adapting and writing language lessons.* Washington, D.C.: Foreign Service Institute.

———. 1976. *Memory, meaning and method: Some psychological perspectives on language learning.* Rowley, Mass.: Newbury House.

———. 1981. Learning a foreign language: The natural ways. In *On TESOL 81,* ed. M. Hines and W. Rutherford, Washington, D.C.: TESOL, 1982.

Strevens, P. 1977. *New orientations in the teaching of English.* Oxford: Oxford University Press.

———. 1980. *Teaching English as an international language.* Oxford: Pergamon Press.

Valdes, J. ed. 1986. *Culture bound: Bridging the cultural gap in language teaching.* New York: Cambridge.

West, M. 1953. *A general service list of English words.* London: Longman.

———. 1960. *Teaching English in difficult circumstances.* London: Longman.

Widdowson, H. 1978. *Teaching language as communication.* Oxford: Oxford University Press.

———. 1983. *Language purpose and language use.* Oxford: Oxford University Press.

Wilkins, D. 1976. *Notional syllabus.* London: Oxford University Press.

Winitz, H. ed. 1981. *A comprehension approach to foreign language teaching.* Rowley, Mass.: Newbury House.

Winitz, H., and Reeds, J. 1975. *Comprehension and problem solving as strategies for language training.* The Hague: Mouton.

4

Assessment: Where Are They Starting? How Are They Progressing?

Barbara A. Humak
Julia A. Spinthourakis

ASSESSMENT IS A critical area in adult ESL. A student who is asked to work above his or her level will become frustrated and discouraged; one who begins working below the appropriate level will be bored and probably upset by the lack of progress. In either case, there is a danger that the student will stop coming to class. The following overview shows when and how assessment tests can be used to ensure an appropriate level of instruction.

Appropriate and meaningful assessment, as either a formal or an informal activity, is an essential element in any learning experience. You have to know what students know before you can teach them what they don't know. You also need some means of measuring progress and obtaining feedback on your own performance as a teacher so that you can, if need be, adapt.

ESL assessment tests are available both for adults who can read and write and for those who cannot. The tests can be administered by a psychologist, a guidance counselor, a classroom teacher, a supervising teacher, or even a trained aide or volunteer. The specific test will prescribe the parameters within which it is to be administered. An ESL test traditionally measures only the non-native speaker's English language ability compared with that of a native English speaker. Most tests will indicate that a student falls into one of the following six broad categories:

1. low beginner

2. high beginner

3. low intermediate

4. high intermediate

5. low advanced

6. high advanced

ESL tests are not intended to assess grade level or intelligence. Although administrators may request grade levels, it must be emphasized that currently no ESL test provides grade-level classifications.

WHAT KINDS OF TESTS ARE USED?

Proficiency tests are used as an initial assessment to define a student's level of language competence or to provide an individual benchmark regarding a specific type of instruction or employment. They may be used to determine students' readiness to undertake a certain subject, where they should be placed, and what they need to work on.

These tests focus on oral or written English and, within those categories, on comprehension or production. Examine test descriptions carefully to choose the appropriate instrument or combination of instruments.

You can also use the following tests of assessment:

Prognostic or aptitude tests which predict a student's probability of success in learning English.

Progress tests which measure the level of mastery of the language in class and the language lab.

Achievement tests, given after formal instruction which measure how well the language has been learned. Prepared locally or by an outside group of examiners, they may be norm-referenced (students' scores are compared with statewide or national averages) or criterion-referenced (students' achievement is rated against specified objectives).

WHAT ARE THE TESTS COMPOSED OF?

While testing techniques vary widely, certain types of activities are fairly common. In a test of **listening comprehension,** for example, students might be asked to answer questions about themselves, their families, or their work; or they might listen to a tape or a passage read by the test administrator and respond to questions. The test administrator may ask them to repeat dictated words or sentences or follow oral instructions such as, "Please stand up," or "Place the pen on the desk."

Assessment of **oral production** may also involve responses to questions about self, family, work, and other common topics. For this type of test, students may view pictures or videotapes and be asked to describe objects or actions or to respond to questions.

Common techniques for assessing **reading comprehension** are much more familiar, for all teachers have encountered reading comprehension assessment on standardized tests. The most widespread means is, of course, having students read a passage and answer questions about it. Sentence completion from a given list of choices; cloze exercises, in which students use context to fill in the blanks; and selection of antonyms and synonyms are other techniques often used to assess reading comprehension.

Written production at a very low level may be assessed by having a student write the names of objects or fill out a form with basic information such as name and address. At intermediate levels, a student can be asked to write short sentences or take dictation. A higher-level student might write a paragraph or an essay that reflects appropriate grammar, usage, and vocabulary.

This list is by no means complete; it represents merely the types of tasks students may be asked to perform. The complexity and difficulty of the tasks will vary depending on the targeted language level.

A note about test preparation: If your students are taking an oral test, preparation is not of great concern. Before they take written tests, however, many of them will need to learn some things about test-taking the American way.

Many foreign students learned by rote, and their test-taking consisted simply of giving back material to the instructor verbatim. Such students have never been exposed to test items like multiple choice, matching, true/false, and fill-in-the-blank. Using a no. 2 pencil to fill in circles on a machine-scored answer sheet can totally baffle them. The American way of testing is culturally unique. A good resource book that you can use to teach your students American test-taking is *How to Take Standardized Tests* (Oliver 1981).

WHICH PLACEMENT TESTS ARE MOST APPROPRIATE?

The tests listed and described in the table are especially appropriate for ESL students with limited educational backgrounds and low levels of ability in English.

Below are other English language tests you may want to use to place adult ESL students:

1. Structure Tests of English Language (STEL)

2. Listening Comprehension Group Tests (LCGT):
    Listening Comprehension Written Test (LCWT)
    Listening Comprehension Picture Test (LCPT)

3. Ilyin Oral Interview (IOI)

4. English Language Skills Assessment (ELSA)

Of these four tests, only the Ilyin Oral Interview requires individual administration. The rest may be given in a group setting. For more information on tests, contact Newbury House Publishers, Inc. (10 East 53rd St., New York, N.Y., 10022).

In adult education, a combination of tests is often used to measure students' English language ability. For example, the Delta Oral Proficiency Test and the literacy section of the BEST work well together. The Delta is particularly good because it is easy to administer and score, and it places a student into either an ESL or an ABE class. The BEST literacy section complements the Adult Performance Level skills around which most competency-based ABE programs are built.

The tests described to this point are designed primarily for students with very low levels of English proficiency. There are, however, many students who function well above the survival level and yet are not proficient enough to exit the basic skills program. For these students, tests such as the Delta may be too rudimentary, producing skewed results and limiting your ability to diagnose and prescribe realistic placement. Several appropriate tests for higher-level students are the Michigan Test of English Language Proficiency (MTELP), the Michigan English Language Aptitude Battery (MELAB), the Comprehensive English Language Test (CELT), and the Test of English as a Foreign Language (TOEFL). Each includes measures of listening, reading,

ESL Placement Tests

Test	Description	Administration
The John Test, LINC Publications	Assesses oral English proficiency. Student is rated on accuracy of information, syntactic structure, fluency, pronunciation. Asks 11 questions about a set of pictures. Student is asked to respond to questions about the accompanying pictures, then retell the complete story, and finally make questions out of statements.	Individual interview Materials: Picture cards, score sheets, instruction sheet Time: 5–15 minutes
The HELP Test, Alemany Press	Tests adult learners who have minimal or no oral English skills and who fall into one of the following categories: (1) no reading skills in any language, (2) minimal reading and writing skills in their native language (less than 4 years of schooling), or (3) non-Roman alphabet background.	Individual interview Materials: Score sheets, picture cards, alphabet chips, telephone Time: 30 minutes
The BEST Test, Center for Applied Linguistics	Tests elementary listening comprehension, speaking, reading, and writing of basic functional skills. Contains two parts: (1) oral/aural and (2) reading/writing.	Oral/aural: individual, 15 minutes Reading/writing: group, 1 hour Materials: Score sheets, set of pictures, literacy booklet
Bilingual Vocational Oral Proficiency Test, Melton, Pennsylvania	Tests listening and speaking skills using both vocabulary and language structures from day-to-day English. Contains four parts: (1) answering questions, (2) describing pictures, (3) imitating, (4) following directions.	Individual Materials: Picture set, score sheets, cups, and saucers Time: 20–30 minutes

Test	Description	Administration
	Test results indicate if student has low, medium, or high level of ability to speak English.	
The Delta Oral Proficiency Test, Delta Systems	Placement test	Individual
	Student answers questions about series of pictures	Materials: Picture booklet, score sheets
	Test results will place student in a beginning, intermediate, or advanced ESL class or more advanced instruction, such as an adult basic education (ABE) class.	Time: 5 minutes
The NICE, The University of the State of New York, The State Education Department	A placement test to determine the level of ESL students entering adult education programs. Provides for an oral warm-up and oral assessment. Includes a basic English literacy screening section.	Individual Materials: Student information sheet, test booklet, picture cue booklet Time: 10–15 minutes
The ESL/Literacy Scale (ELS), Academic Therapy Publications	An assessment tool for quickly identifying the appropriate level for ESL and literacy instruction. Subtests include listening comprehension, grammar, life skills, reading comprehension.	Individual oral screening; remainder of test group-administered Time: 15–20 minutes

vocabulary, and grammar (and recently, measures of writing on the MELAB and the TOEFL).

WHAT ABOUT PROGRESS TESTS?

Both students and instructors need feedback. Progress tests given during an ESL course can provide such feedback. The information obtained will help you meet the individual needs of your students as well as satisfy administrators who want to see where the program is going. Since progress tests must measure what the student has learned, their content is based on the curriculum.

You can informally encourage students to assess their own language growth by giving them questions to answer about their language abilities. For a beginning student, the questions can be written in the student's native language. Given when students begin an ESL course and again when the course is completed, the student self-diagnostic survey usually reflects language growth and can also show where each student feels more work is needed. Students also enjoy self-check exercises for specialized vocabulary, listening comprehension, grammar exercises, and reading comprehension questions.

As for formal tests, those that are commercially available are not often satisfactory as progress tests. There are too many variables in local situations: reasons for testing, the variety of skill areas to test, and curricular emphases and sequence, for example. Consequently, adapting an existing test or developing a new one based on local program goals and materials is usually preferable.

To prepare a progress test, consider the following steps:

1. Identify the skill areas taught—listening, speaking, reading, and writing.

2. Identify the vocabulary, structures, situations, and functions taught.

3. Develop items that test the skill areas (number 1) and the language aspects (number 2).

4. Check to make sure that the test items correspond to the levels of the curriculum.

A review checklist for ESL tests that you may want to apply to any locally constructed tests can be found in "Second Language Testing" (Cohen 1979).

Whatever method of progress testing you use, the results will help the instructors and administrators in your program group and regroup classes by identifying areas of progress and weakness. In addition, progress tests can provide an incentive for your students. They are a concrete means of showing them their developing mastery of the English language.

Bibliography

Alderson, J. C.; Krahnke, K. J.; and Stansfield, C. W., eds. 1987. *Reviews of English language proficiency tests.* Washington, D. C.: TESOL International.

Briere, E. J., and Hinofotis, F. B., eds. 1979. *Concepts in language testing.* Washington, D.C.: TESOL International.

Cohen, A. 1979. Second language testing. In *Teaching English as a second or foreign language,* ed. M. Celce-Murcia and L. McIntosh. Rowley, Mass.: Newbury House.

Oliver, Charles. 1981. *How to take standardized tests.* Englewood Cliffs, N.J.: Prentice-Hall.

Oller, J. W., ed. 1983. *Issues in language testing research.* Rowley, Mass.: Newbury House.

CHAPTER

5

Preparing Lesson Plans

F. Anne Mock

CHRISTOPHER COLUMBUS WAS *fortunate indeed when he traveled to the New World. Consider the facts:*

· *He didn't know where he was going.*

· *When he got there, he didn't know where he was.*

· *When he got back, he wasn't sure where he had been.*

· *He made his whole trip on borrowed money, and it made him famous.*

Now that's lucky!

Luck is bound to come along once in a while, but if you want your ESL students to make important discoveries each day they are in your class, lesson plans are a must. Lesson plans are the final stage of lesson preparation. Before you can create them, you already know where your students are (assessment), where they need to be (goals), and what part of that progress you plan to attain in the class session (lesson objectives or competencies). The lesson plan simply details how you are going to accomplish those objectives. This chapter provides a detailed guide for developing good, complete lesson plans.

WHY ARE LESSON PLANS IMPORTANT?

Lesson plans are important in any teaching activity, but they are especially critical in ESL classes for several reasons.

33

First, in an ESL class the teacher must control language carefully so that it can be understood and subsequently used by the students. Language must be limited to that which is essential to achieving an objective or a competency. For a teacher, this necessity means deciding beforehand the specific linguistic purpose of each class as well as ways to achieve that purpose most efficiently.

Second, an ESL lesson should include four stages: (1) **preparation** of students to receive the new material, (2) **presentation** of new material by the teacher, (3) **practice** by students under teacher direction, and (4) **production**, or use of the new language by each student in a summarizing, creative, or spontaneous situation. In some cases, teaching stops at the presentation stage; very often teachers neglect to go beyond the practice stage. Too little time is given to the real production of language in the typical classroom. Making a lesson plan serves to emphasize the four stages and guarantees that your classroom activities will follow this "4P" sequence.

The final and perhaps most vital reason for planning each ESL lesson is to meet as directly as possible the urgent needs of your ESL students. Lesson plans should reflect their recognized needs, not the pages of an assigned text.

Although you probably conduct some type of needs assessment at the beginning of a course, you'll want to continue to gather information throughout it. As you and your students come to know and trust each other, they will more freely communicate important personal and cultural information. If you set aside a brief but special time for students to talk about themselves and for other students to ask questions and comment, you'll get a clear idea of your students' language and cultural needs. Other classroom activities that provide material for language lessons are journal writing and daily activity charts (simple lists of what was done). As communication flows and grows within your classroom, your lesson plans can reflect students' thoughts and feelings as well as their practical needs.

TWO PHASES OF LESSON PLANNING

Although a lesson plan is usually considered to be a list of the strategies used in the classroom, those strategies depend on important decisions that must be made before the actual activities can be planned: *What* will be the content of the lesson? What specific aspects can be adequately covered within the given time frame? What vocabulary, grammatical structures, and language skills are needed? Only after these questions are answered can we move to *how* this content will be taught. Therefore, ESL lesson planning has two phases.

The Content of the Lesson: Phase 1

Five choices concerning content must be made before classroom activities are planned. As familiarity with the selection process grows, the decisions come more easily and quickly. You must select:

1. A **topic** of interest and of use to students (for example, tools used on the job)

2. A **competency** involving the topic (for example, how to locate tools, understand their use, or report their condition)

3. The **language skills**—listening, speaking, reading, and/or writing—that are needed to achieve the competency

4. The **vocabulary** and **structures** essential to the competency

5. The **materials** (such as books, visuals, and actual objects) necessary to teach the competency effectively. These may be teacher-made, published, or adaptations of consumer materials, such as catalogs.

This selection establishes the groundwork for the four stages of the lesson: preparation, presentation, practice, and production. A chart for Phase 1 of lesson planning and a sample chart are on pages 36–37.

Classroom Activities: Phase 2

The second phase deals with the "how" of the lesson—the activities and strategies that you will use to help students achieve communicative competence in the selected content area. You need to decide how you will lead students through the four *P*'s:

Stage 1. Preparation: If possible, tie in the new material with topics or language covered previously. Questions might be asked to elicit students' knowledge in the area; a short role-playing session might set the stage. Ideally, the preparation provides a "hook" to capture student interest and focus it on the topic. Cultural points needed to understand the new material should also be included.

Stage 2. Presentation: You can present the new material (decided upon in phase 1) to the class through visuals, a reading, or a dialogue until students understand the purpose of the lesson.

Stage 3. Practice: Students can practice the new material, or competency, through choral repetition, individual repetition, question and

Lesson Plan: Phase 1

Topic	Competency	Language Skills	Vocabulary	Structures	Materials

Sample Lesson Plan: Phase 1

Topic	Competency	Language Skills	Vocabulary	Structures	Materials
Tools	identify tools by name	listening and speaking	hammer saw pliers screwdriver lathe, etc get take give where	It's a ——. They're ——. Where is the —— ? Verb *be* Contractions Commands Singular vs. plural	catalog of tools real tools *Oxford Picture Dictionary*

Lesson Plan: Phase 2

Competency: _____
Activities:
 1. **Preparation**

 2. **Presentation**

 3. **Practice**

 4. **Production**

answer, oral drills, listening exercises, or reading and writing drills.
Practice should continue until you feel all the students have acquired
the competency.

Stage 4. Production: Give each student the chance to produce or use
the language competency in a new, nonpractice situation. This may
be performing role play; doing an oral or a written exercise; identifying words from visuals; following simple or complex instructions;
paraphrasing or summarizing; taking dictation; reading words, sentences, or paragraphs; or doing cloze exercises. This final stage is particularly important in an ESL classroom. If students leave class at the
practice stage, they will lack the confidence and the experience to use
the language in the outside world.
    A blank chart for completing phase 2 of a lesson plan appears above,
and a sample chart appears on page 39.
    Phases 1 and 2 represent two sequential steps in the process of plan-
ning an ESL lesson. If you're an experienced teacher, you may not need
to put both phases down in writing. If the "what" of the lesson is al-

Sample Lesson Plan: Phase 2

Competency: <u>Identify tools by name</u>

Activities:

1. **Preparation**

   Brief skit (live or on videotape) depicting various items breaking. "Victim" uses hands and other ineffective means to try to fix them and becomes frustrated.

2. **Presentation**

   Use realia:
   a. Present tools (in conjunction with appropriate part of video if possible).
   b. Ask questions and respond.
   c. Give commands and respond.
   d. Ask questions; students respond.
   e. Give commands; students respond.

3. **Practice**

   a. Student points out tool as teacher speaks (statement and question).
   b. Students ask questions of other students.
   c. Students follow simple and complex commands.

4. **Production**

   a. Give complete commands to each student.
   b. Students respond individually.
   c. Students give each other commands.

ready clear in your mind, you may want to move immediately to phase 2 and develop the activities for teaching the competency. Phase 1 is especially appropriate if you feel the sequence of activities (the "how") is by now almost automatic but want to remind yourself to control the vocabulary and structure of the lesson. If you are a beginning ESL teacher, on the other hand, you'd do well to put both phases of the process in writing.

Before the four stages of each new lesson, you should review the previous day's lesson. Beyond the four stages lies the possibility of expanding the lesson. Expansion can be accomplished by tasks that take students into the community to experiment with their new language competence. It can involve moving to a supplementary text with a reading, an anecdote, a cartoon, or a dialogue involving the same or a similar competency. There may also be a natural expansion into the cultural connotation of the competency. If the competency has caught on and is important to your students, follow it wherever it leads.

6

The Whys and Ways of Practice

Jeffrey P. Bright

THE FIRST JOB of an ESL teacher is to make sure that students understand *the English presented in class. The second and no less important task is to enable students to* use *that English to communicate. The only sure route to skill and confidence in language use is through practice, yet language drills can be as appealing as dentists' drills unless they are varied. Three general types of practice are explained in this chapter to help you attain that essential variety.*

It can happen in any ESL class: students act as if yesterday's lesson never took place. They cannot use the language material—the commands, dialogue, and vocabulary—you presented the day before. Admittedly, some reasons for nonlearning are beyond your control as a teacher, such as students' having little or no contact with comprehensible English outside of class. But you *can* foster more solid learning *by providing more varied and effective practice* while students are in your class.

If you have never before taught ESL, you may underestimate the need for repetition. Yet using language is a skill, not unlike the skills of word processing, carpentry, tailoring, and the like. And skills are, by their very nature, mastered only through practice. In language learning, three kinds of practice lead to competence: (1) familiarity practice, (2) skill-building practice, and (3) skill-using practice. Practice of all three types belongs in each day's lesson.

EASING THEM IN: FAMILIARITY PRACTICE

Familiarity practice aims to ease learners into new language material. Repetition through multiple listening, speaking, and reading activities is the most common form of familiarity practice. For example, in a lesson developed around a Total Physical Response (TPR) sequence, a teacher may say and act out commands several times before students silently perform the actions themselves. Only after much practice to ensure comprehension are they expected to say the commands themselves. Familiarity with the sounds, vocabulary, word order, and other features of English develops through these multiple, nonthreatening exposures to the language. In both group and individual repetition, the teacher who gives a noncritical and reassuring echo after students' efforts is also providing valuable familiarity practice. Once is never enough in teaching and learning language skills. Familiarity practice conditions the learner for further language growth.

A variety of familiarity practice exercises are described below. Many others have been developed by creative teachers. You can use these as a base and experiment to find others that work well with your students.

1. Aural repetition (multiple listenings) with or without accompanying aids such as actions, pictures, realia, charts, and written language.

2. Oral repetition (multiple speakings) by the whole class, by groups (male-female, half of room), or by individuals (volunteers, peer-selected, teacher-selected), with or without teacher echo after student attempts.

3. Listening focused on meaning. Students listen and—
   a. point to the word or words said,
   b. say the number of the picture described,
   c. circle the object named, or
   d. perform the action requested.

4. Listening focused on form. Students listen to—
   a. pairs of words/sentences/questions and say, "Same" or "Different."
   b. trios of words/sentences/questions and say which is different (1, 2, or 3).

    c. utterances and count the number of words in each.

    d. a list of utterances and indicate which of several key words each contains (such as question words: *what, when,* and *where*).

5. Progressive comprehension questions. For a given lesson, students listen and answer first "yes" or "no" questions, then gradually progress to questions such as "how many," "what," and "who."

SKILL-BUILDING PRACTICE

It has been said that half of the language taught in ESL is questions and the other half is answers. There is a kernel of truth in that oversimplification. Yet time spent in active skill-building practice helps take learners and teacher closer to the goal of skill mastery. Typically, a skill-building exercise has three elements:

1. **Language material**—a set of related sentences, questions, or vocabulary items with which students are already familiar or which you can cue for them on the spot.

2. **Language practice process**—an activity such as substituting a new word for an existing one in a sentence, asking and answering questions, selecting the right word to complete a sentence, or putting scrambled words in order according to a remembered model.

3. **Classroom activity**—teacher-student or student-student exchanges, silent independent work, or group collaboration through which students are supported and guided step-by-step to make a good many utterances.

    Teachers who use traditional textbooks should take into account that skill-building practice goes beyond the structural drill. Adult ESL students need to learn to use language in ways that cannot be squeezed into the mold of a substitution drill. Consider just a few examples of skill-building practice. The lesson topic could be establishing and maintaining social contact with a person. Specific exchanges (for instance, "How's it going?" "Fine. How about you?" "O.K." could be presented as short situational dialogues. After familiarity practice, several skill-building exercises could be used:

1. Teacher-conducted question-answer drill: Answers are given by teacher *or* students.

2. Chain or circle drill: Student A and student B engage in the dialogue, then student B and student C, and so on.

3. Two-line drill: The class divides into two lines facing each other. Students in the first line begin the dialogue, and their partners in the second line respond. When finished, the students in the first line all move down one person to face a new partner. (The one at the end comes to the head of the line.) Practice resumes, with students in the second line beginning the dialogue. This activity could also be done with two circles—one inner, one outer—facing each other.

4. Jigsaw dyads: Working in pairs, students refer to special worksheets. Student A starts off with question 1, which is printed only on his or her worksheet. Student B must respond. Then student B starts question 2, which is only on B's worksheet, and so forth.

5. Cloze, or fill-in-the-blank, exercises: students fill in a blank with (a) an exact word presented earlier in the lesson, (b) one of several possible choices provided, or (c) any word, phrase, or sentence that fits. In the sample lesson, the last word of each line of the dialogue could be deleted, for example.

From these examples, you can see that skill-building activities are basically *multiple* and *varied* opportunities to practice *limited* amounts of language in *highly structured* activities. These characteristics help ensure success. For other types of lessons, skill-building practice could utilize other media:

- charts (maps, schedules, grids)
- flash cards (to put in order)
- pictures (individual or in sequence)
- real objects
- Language Master cards (cards with words and illustrations that, when slipped into a machine, cause the word to be pronounced)
- cassette recordings, computers, or other technology

SKILL-USING PRACTICE

With the third type of practice—skill-*using*—you move your students further along the language-teaching continuum from controlled to free activity. Here are some examples of skill-using activities:

1. "Fruit basket upset" (so named by Adena Staben, College of Lake County, Grayslake, Illinois): Prepare 3 x 5 cards with questions

and corresponding answers—enough cards so that each person in class gets one. Students must mingle, saying and listening to each other's items until everyone has found a match that makes sense with his or her card.

2. Information gap: Using specially constructed materials, students work in pairs—but without looking at each other's papers—to solve an information puzzle. Each student has only half the information, such as the names of stores on a street map, times on a schedule, or prices for pictured items. The students ask each other questions to complete the information on their papers. Or two students work back to back so that they cannot see each other's papers or desks. Student A has objects, pictures, or cards with words representing such things as jobs, people, or food arranged on a grid or desk. Student B has the same items but unarranged. A tells B, B asks A, or both, until B's arrangement is the same.

3. Find someone who . . . : To give practice with almost any type of question, provide students with copies of a lead-in and a list of possible completions, as many as (or fewer than) there are people in your class. Students must circulate and ask questions until they find someone who can answer yes to a given question. The one who answers yes signs his or her name on a blank line next to that item on the questioner's paper. (The usual rule is only one signature from any one other student on a paper.) The "winner" is the one who first fills all the blanks on the paper with different students' signatures, but, in reality, all the students are winners because they have been involved in enjoyable, realistic practice.

    A given day's practice can focus on verb tenses if you prepare a list that calls for that tense. For the present perfect tense, for example, the list could start off like this:

Have you ever
                had a massage? _____
                lived in a very hot climate? _____
                painted the outside of a house? _____

For the past tense, the list could include the following:

Find someone who
                worked overtime this week. _____
                watched TV last night. _____
                moved within the last year. _____

This list calls for questions beginning with *did:* "Did you work overtime this week?" and so on. The list can also be organized by life-skill topics or include idioms studied the day before. The possibilities are almost endless.

4. Class interview: A student sits in front of the class. The others compose oral and written questions that he or she must answer. Be sure you do not ask students to do this activity before they are ready, and be prepared to act as a referee if the questions are asked at too high a level.

Guided role play, open-ended stories, and more complex information gaps and jigsaw configurations are also examples of skill-using practice activities. What they have in common is that they call upon students to *use* the language they have been learning—employing not merely their powers of recall but also their judgment and ability to recombine and create new arrangements from familiar language items. In contrast, familiarity practice fosters comprehension and recognition but very little recall. Skill-building exercises lie in between; they call for manipulating and matching, choosing from limited alternatives, and repeating to make sure the item is well learned.

Each type of practice has its role in developing language competence. The exercises described here, and many more, are available to you as tools to use in helping your students meet their goals. There is both a challenge and a pleasure in devising and delivering lessons that provide the practice students need for language mastery.

Bibliography

Center for Applied Linguistics. (no date; c. 1983). *English as a second language resource manual.* Washington, D.C.: published by author.

Escobar, J. S., and McKeon, D. 1979. Four phases of the teaching and learning of a second language. In *The adult basic education TESL handbook.* ed. D. E. Bartley. New York: Collier Macmillan.

Messerschmidt, D. S. 1981. *Listening for structural cues with the mini-check system.* San Francisco: Alemany Press.

Moran, P. 1983. Lesson planning. In *Shifting gears: Hands-on activities for learning workplace skills and English as a second language.* Brattleboro, Vt.: The Experiment in International Living.

Olsen, J. E. W. 1977. *Communication starters.* San Francisco: Alemany Press.

Rivers, W. M., and Temperley, M. S. 1978. *A practical guide to teaching English as a second or foreign language.* New York: Oxford University Press.

Stevick, E. W. 1982. *Teaching and learning languages.* New York: Cambridge University Press.

C H A P T E R

7

Teaching the Multilevel Class

Faye Van Arsdall Schmelig

VARIETY MAY BE the spice of life, but it also is responsible for a great deal of the challenge facing an ESL teacher. Varying cultures, native languages, ages, educational backgrounds, and needs as well as abilities commonly confront the teacher. Meeting the challenge of such a multilevel class is the focus of this chapter.

Every teacher knows intuitively that there is no such thing as a homogeneous class. No two individuals learn in the same way. Teachers of adults are perhaps more keenly aware of these differences in learners and learning styles because of the obvious diversity in the ages of their students, the degrees of literacy skills and educational backgrounds, and the wide range of life experiences represented in the adult classroom.

Adult ESL teachers face an even greater challenge in meeting the individual needs of their students, for they often must deal not only with students from various cultural and ethnic backgrounds, but with students who speak different languages entirely. It is not at all unusual to find, in the same ESL classroom, students with a very wide range

The material in this chapter was prepared for an Adult Education Act 310 grant publication.

of English proficiency. Even in situations where students are carefully tested and placed, some students at a given level may be quite proficient at speaking, for example, yet weak in reading or writing skills.

Another factor that contributes greatly to the multilevel challenge is the open-entry, open-exit system characteristic of many adult learning centers. With students entering a class at any time during a term, new students who test out at a particular level are likely to find themselves far below the actual level of the other students, even when they enter the class after only a few days. *Every* language class is, therefore, a multilevel one, and every good teacher is constantly trying to meet the needs of each individual student. One way to meet these diverse needs is through individualized instruction.

INDIVIDUALIZATION

What exactly is individualized instruction? Perhaps it is easier to define what individualization is *not*. Individualized instruction is not isolating people. It is not separating students into discrete groups and keeping them there all the time. Language learning *demands* interaction. The very essence of language involves communication—speaking, listening, gesturing, moving and other ways of interacting with other human beings.

In fact, individualized *learning* might be a more appropriate term than individualized instruction, for in reality, a teacher is only a channel through which individuals can learn. If the teacher supplies a nonthreatening environment, caring guidance, and effective resources, individualized learning can take place.

USING RESOURCES TO ACHIEVE INDIVIDUALIZATION

Books, machines, handouts, and activity packets can all be vehicles for individualized learning, but all the fancy equipment that money can buy will not individualize a program. Neither does successful individualization require genius-level organizational skills. What it does require is becoming aware of and using *all* the resources at hand—and they include not only the adult center and all its personnel but also, and especially, the students.

Even a teacher's weakness can, in fact, become an asset to a program. A teacher who, for example, is threatened by operating a movie projector will probably find a student who loves to operate projectors or perhaps two or three students in the class willing to learn how. Could there be a better task-oriented activity than to have these students go to the library to learn from the media specialist how to operate a piece of equipment, then come back to the classroom to demonstrate what they have learned? Or what more practical reading exercise could there be than to provide the instruction booklet and have a small group of students figure it out?

Students can help with the organization of the individualized classroom and learn valuable skills at the same time. Small groups or pairs may volunteer to take attendance and keep other routine paperwork up to date by acting as class secretaries. Others may help set up a learning center by collecting pictures to illustrate a list of vocabulary words or specific situations recently encountered in an assigned reading. Students may also learn while contributing to the class by making flash cards, creating their own learning games and activities, dictating spelling words or simple sentences to each other, or even typing handouts or transcribing tapes of dialogues that the class has created.

In many cases of successful individualized learning, students have taught each other. In fact, students often learn better from a peer than from someone in the position of teacher. A student who has recently learned a particular language skill is often the perfect person to explain it most effectively to a new learner; and by teaching it to someone else, the tutor reviews and strengthens his or her own skill.

PAIRING AND GROUPING

Certainly independent work is a vital practice in the individualized classroom, but the larger question should be how to establish rapport and cooperation. That is especially true in an ESL classroom, given the natural fear and isolation that many of these learners experience. Yet you will recognize immediately the difficulty in planning for a cohesive lesson where each student feels a part of the larger group while at the same time meets his or her own needs.

Variety in forming groups and pairs is one answer. One day you may begin with a large group activity, then gradually break the class into smaller and smaller units as the lesson progresses. The following day you might decide to begin with small groups or pairs in preparation for a large group discussion or activity. On other days or during set times each day, you may choose to assign small group projects and have the groupings remain fixed for their duration.

Varying the ways in which you divide the large class will help bring out the individual potential of each student and, if carefully planned, can establish a feeling of harmony within the larger group. The following suggestions are offered as a starting point to illustrate some of the different possibilities.

1. Similar skill levels: More fluent students, for example, may discuss a specific topic while you work with the less verbal students. Or while the beginners complete a basic writing assignment, you can work on advanced writing skills with the more proficient writers.

To keep independent groups on the task, be sure to give clear directions and specific objectives. For example, instead of asking a discussion group to talk about the problems of older citizens, you might create a case study similar to the example below and explain that each small group must agree on one single solution to the problem.

> *Situation:* Jean Williams is a widow. Her husband died three years ago, and for the first time in her life she had to go to work to support her two children. She works the late shift from four to midnight in a restaurant. Her daughter, Jana, is fifteen and will graduate from high school in two years. Her son, Louis, has just started his first year at the junior college. He has a part-time job but still lives at home. Six months ago, Jean's mother, who is seventy-three and also a widow, moved into their small apartment. Her behavior has become a problem for the whole family. In many ways she is like a child, and she needs a lot of care and attention. Jana and Louis have tried to be kind and patient, but the problem has just become too difficult for them. Last week they told their mother that if their grandmother had to live with them they were both going to leave home.
>
> *Problem:* You are Jean Williams. What are you going to do?

Problematic situations dealing with such topics as age, divorce, male-female roles, and child abuse generally ignite a very lively discussion even without your presence to stimulate the group. Although creating these story problems can be half the fun and can, indeed, be an effective project for advanced students, several excellent resources for this type of discussion are available. Some of the best are *React/Interact: Situations for Communication* (Byrd and Clemente-Cabetas 1980), *Can't Stop Talking* (Rooks 1983), and *The Non-Stop Discussion Workbook* (Rooks 1981).

2. Different skill levels: As mentioned earlier, students often learn better from peers than from a teacher. An advanced student can tutor individuals or small groups. For example, a student who has mastered the past tense could explain and practice it with a small group of beginners. This type of grouping or pairing is useful in dealing with new arrivals to the class or students who have been absent. Take care, however, not to place the same students in the role of tutor all the time. Even beginning learners can introduce a new student and help explain class routine, and a beginner who has mastered a particular point can tutor another beginner who needs further practice.

3. Similar interests: Regardless of their ability levels, students who have something in common usually have much to communicate to each other. Meeting and talking to others with similar interests can often establish bonds between students that, in turn, help unify the larger group and create a sharing, learning atmosphere. Friendships may also develop and extend beyond the classroom to ease the cultural shock and adjustment of an ESL student.

As an example, students who plan to enter a U.S. college can do a group project, or those who live with American families can get together to discuss the problems and benefits. Women with small children can work together on activities related to child care. Persons who hope to work in similar jobs can practice vocabulary and grammatical structures related to that line of work. The possibilities are unlimited.

4. Random groupings: Sometimes grouping students completely at random leads to enjoyable, interesting, and surprisingly effective results. Random grouping not only affords an excellent way for students to get to know each other, it also provides a way to group students of different ability levels without focusing on the roles of tutor and tutee. (Students recognize such labeling all too quickly.) By using a variety of methods to form random groupings, you can also heighten the interest level and add "pizzaz" to the activity. A few suggestions follow as a springboard for other ideas.

   a. Have the large group count off, for example, from one to six. All the ones will form one group, the twos another, and so on.

   b. In a hat place pieces of construction paper of as many different colors as there will be groups. Ask each student to choose a favorite color. Students will then group themselves by color.

   c. From a mail-order catalog or the Sunday advertising supplements to the newspaper, cut items from different sections or departments of a store. Give one picture to each student, and then ask students to group themselves according to specified categories, such as housewares, clothing, or hardware.

   d. Observe what students are wearing on a particular day and group them accordingly. For example, everyone wearing jeans will form one group, skirts or shorts another, dresses or pants still another.

   e. Simply allow students to group themselves. You might also list four or five different activities and invite students to choose the activity they prefer.

5. Pairing: At times you'll want the whole class or certain students to work in pairs rather than groups. Some pronunciation exercises, for

example, are better suited to pair work. Students of similar or different ability levels can be paired in much the same way as for forming groups. Choosing the way students are paired, however, is more important, since one student in a pair may tend to dominate. Variety is, again, the key!

RESOURCE LABS AND LEARNING CENTERS

Developing learning centers where students can choose among different activities is a popular and effective method of meeting the multilevel challenge. One section of the classroom can be set up, for example, as a listening/pronunciation center, where students work with the Language Master and tape recorders. Special tables or sections of the room can be organized for grammar, reading, or writing. There could also be an area where games—commercial as well as teacher-made or student-made—are stored and played. A conversation center can be organized with a box of suggested topics and speaking activities to choose from.

Organizing and developing materials for such learning centers cannot be done overnight. However, with a plan in mind, a few cardboard boxes, and some file folders, you can collect materials and exercises in an amazingly short period of time. Keep in mind *student goals* when gathering and developing the materials. Many activities can revolve around basic survival skills and vocabulary; others can focus on the types of jobs students hold or hope to hold. With a simple plan as to what centers are needed and where they will be located, you can begin with commercial materials already on hand. As new activities are developed, add them to the appropriate centers. Keeping in mind that these activities will be used over and over again, you may want to protect some items by covering them with clear plastic. It's also a good idea to label or code papers in some way to make filing easy and to prepare answer sheets so that students can self-correct the exercises.

Students themselves may enjoy preparing exercises, activities, or games for the learning centers. Keep on hand a box of supplies such as construction paper, glue, index cards, markers, catalogs, and magazines. Plan projects that students will complete and then add to the centers. The following are suggested activities that students might develop.

1. Flash cards: Provide a list of words and ask students to find pictures illustrating each. On one side of a card, students should write a vocabulary word; on the other side, they should glue the picture. Then place the flash cards in the reading center and use them for sight-word practice.

2. Dictionaries: Suggest general categories, such as fruits, vegetables, clothing, and animals. Ask students to make booklet dictionaries by finding or drawing pictures of items in their assigned category, writing the words and their definitions, and perhaps giving two or three sentences using the words. Then place the dictionaries in a vocabulary learning center for future use.

3. Matching activities: For the reading lab, have students prepare a set of index cards with, for example, ten words written in blue on one set of cards and their antonyms written in red on another set. An answer card could also be included so that students can check their answers after matching up the cards. Other matching exercises can include such things as words with pictures, words with their definitions, time words with verb tenses, and sentence beginnings with sentence endings.

4. Listening exercises: Advanced students may enjoy listening to a tape of a song, a poem, or a reading, and transcribing the words. Once they get all the words down on paper and you have checked them for accuracy, replace every fifth to seventh word with a blank. Then photocopy the transcription and put it into the listening station. Less advanced students can listen to the same tape and fill in the missing words in the transcription.

5. Sequencing: All sorts of excellent sequencing activities can be developed by students. For example, have them cut out cartoons and glue them to index cards with the proper sequence numbered on the backs. Or ask students to write each word of a sentence on a separate index card, shuffle the cards, and put them into envelopes for other students to unscramble. Even short reading selections can be cut up by paragraphs and glued to large index cards for later practice in sequencing.

These learning centers provide a convenient and effective way to personalize learning by allowing students to work at their own pace and at their particular skill level. However, remember that they are not the end-all to individualizing an ESL classroom. They are simply one resource among many to choose from. If overused, learning centers lose their effectiveness.

Variety may be the single most important factor in a multilevel classroom. By varying the types of exercises, activities, and groupings you use, you will heighten interest and motivation, accommodate different learning styles, and provide students with the opportunity to get to know and help each other.

Some of the suggestions listed here may be of use to you, but you and your students are your best resources. Find out what their needs are. Develop your own teaching style. There is room for a great deal of freedom and flexibility in a multilevel situation. When viewed in this light, the multilevel class can become as much of an opportunity as it is a challenge.

Bibliography

Byrd, D., and Clemente-Cabetas, I. 1980. *React/interact: Situations for communication.* New York: Regents.

Center for Applied Linguistics. *Teaching ESL in a multilevel classroom.* Center for Applied Linguistics Refugee Guide. Adult Education Series no. 3.

Rooks, G. 1981. *The non-stop discussion workbook.* Rowley, Mass.: Newbury House.

— — —. 1983. *Can't stop talking.* Rowley, Mass.: Newbury House.

8

Using the Senses in Language Instruction

Lucy Madsen Guglielmino

A COOK WHO is skillful in the use of spices and herbs can create a delightful meal instead of a merely satisfactory one. And a teacher who skillfully uses materials and activities that involve the learners' senses can make an ESL classroom especially dynamic and effective. This chapter pinpoints three kinds of sensory activity you can use to create lively language instruction.

   While frequent repetition in language instruction is essential, it can become quite boring. Adding variety and involving learners beyond simple repetition of a word, phrase, sentence, or even dialogue greatly enhances the impact of instruction. Three kinds of activities that can be used for enjoyable, multisensory practice of essential elements are: exercises set to music, drama and role play, and kinesthetic activities. These activities have many benefits:

   1. They can help students relax. ESL students, living in a country where they do not speak the language (or do not speak it well), are subject to a great deal of stress. They may be discounted or ignored; they face constant frustration as they attempt to arrange for services, buy necessities, or find and hold a job. Any activity that releases some

Portions of this chapter were presented at the Florida Literacy Symposium, on June 11, 1987, in Miami, Florida.

of the tension connected with language difficulties helps remove a potential block to learning.

2. When carefully chosen, the activities can help create a comfortable climate for learning. They not only foster a warm student-teacher relationship but build group cohesiveness as well.

3. Different learning styles or orientations—visual, aural, kinesthetic, right or left hemispheric preference—can be accommodated.

4. Humor is often injected into the classroom, and humor has other virtues besides being enjoyable. Research shows that illustrating learning material with humor increases students' retention rates.

5. The activities provide a change of pace, a break in routine, that enhances attention span.

6. Many of these activities put the *student* in the spotlight rather than the teacher, building the self-confidence necessary for the student to apply newly learned language skills outside the classroom.

7. The activities provide a chance to practice, review, and expand language skills; practice that is more valuable and memorable because it is varied.

One caveat: While these activities can be enjoyable and enhance learning, they can turn into unpleasant experiences if your students are not ready for them. Be sure you prepare them with vocabulary, grammar structures, cultural knowledge, and pronunciation (if necessary). Remember: Your students need success.

THE MAGIC OF MUSIC

Music accompanies our celebrations: parties, weddings, holidays. It sets an atmosphere or reflects a mood when we dance, when we dine, when we worship, and when we mourn. We respond to music physically and emotionally.

Religions have used music to convey and reinforce their teachings throughout the ages. Research based on suggestology, the method of instruction developed by Georgi Lozanov, provides some evidence for the merit of this approach. One of Lozanov's major assumptions is that learning involves both conscious and unconscious functions; optimal learning takes place when there is a "harmonious, relaxed working together of all parts of the learner" (Stevick 1983, p. 16). Lozanov uses baroque music to achieve this state of relaxation and harmony. The music, carefully chosen and timed with the presentation of material, produces an alpha state in which the mind is relaxed but quite receptive to learning (Williams 1983). Research indicates that suggestology is extremely effective, cutting instructional time by two-thirds for a group of Iowa language teachers (Bancroft 1983). The total impact of the Lozanov method cannot be ascribed to music alone, however, since the use of music is only one aspect of that method.

Another reason for music's effectiveness in promoting learning may be that music is processed by the right hemisphere in most individuals (Williams 1983). Since left-brain approaches predominate in most language instruction, music can be a major benefit to learners with a strong right-brain orientation. As the left hemisphere learns the words and the right hemisphere learns the melody and rhythm, songs strengthen retention with this complementary function (Williams 1983).

Of the seven perceptual learning styles identified by James and Galbraith (1984), the use of songs can address five. Learners can see the words (print); hear the words and music (aural); sing the words (interactive); clap, tap their feet, act out the words, or move their bodies to the rhythm of the music (kinesthetic); and view pictures or objects that illustrate the music (visual). Learning through songs and chants, therefore, reaches students through multiple channels and greatly increases the likelihood that an approach suitable to each student's predominant learning style is being used.

Songs and chants are ideal for teaching or reinforcing numerous aspects of language: sounds; rhythm and stress; elisions or reductions (such as *gonna* for *going to*); conversational patterns; language structures such as tenses, comparisons, negatives, and idioms; vocabulary; language functions such as making a complaint, requesting a service, or asking for information; and cultural information.

Songs and chants need to be chosen carefully, however. Their words and structures should closely represent standard spoken English, and their content should be related to a current lesson (unless you're using the song or chant solely for a change of pace or as an enrichment activity). Choose a tune that is easy to learn and easy to sing. (Who can relax while straining to hit a high note?) For beginners or multilevel classes, choose a song with repetitive lyrics or a chorus so that lower-level students can learn the song in a reasonable amount of time. To gain the most from a song or chant, design additional activities around it: a synonym search using the words of the song, class discussion of a cultural point raised in the song, or a dictation, for example.

Current popular songs, old favorites, and folksongs are all possible material for an ESL classroom. A poll of the radio stations listened to by the class will help you choose songs, but you can also compose songs and chants especially appropriate for your group. Guglielmino (1986) describes a situation in a vocation-specific ESL class conducted at a worksite. The students were reluctant to ask their supervisor questions or even to report that machinery was not working correctly, fearing the supervisor would interpret that information as criticism. By no means an accomplished musician, the ESL instructor created a simple jazz chant that provided the students with the language needed to ask for help and to report a malfunction, while reflecting a more casual, open relationship between employee and supervisor. The rhythm was pounded out on a table with the palm of the hand. Reticent as the workers had been, they enjoyed the chant, assimilated its message, and learned essential vocabulary and structures.

You don't feel ready to jump right in and create songs and chants from scratch? You know your singing voice is not exactly the greatest? Don't rule out songs and chants yet. Several excellent songbooks and cassettes have been developed especially for ESL classes; among these are *Jazz Chants* (Graham 1978), *Turn of the Century Songbook* (Graham 1982), and *Small Talk* (Graham 1986). Cassette tapes are available for use with each book. All the chants and songs were written by Graham for ESL students, so their language and structures are appropriate. Instructions to the teacher and a key to the structures presented in each chant are provided. The *Turn of the Century Songbook* also includes exercises to accompany each tune. Graham's songs help remedy some very difficult problems for English-language learners in an entertaining way. For example, "She Washes the Dishes and Puts Them Away" works on the often-confusing *s* problem in verb tenses and plurals. Contrary to the title, this is not a sexist chant. In the second verse, *he* washes the dishes and puts them away, and in the third verse, *they* take care of those unending dishes together. In the final verse, both have had enough. They break all the dishes and throw them away. The unexpected twist adds humor and keeps interest high.

Like *Turn of the Century Songbook, Tune in to English* (Kind 1980) gives new words to traditional tunes. Each song addresses a particular use of language, such as asking for an item at a store or introducing oneself. Exercises, music, and an index to structures are provided; an audiocassette is also available.

Advanced students might enjoy *If You Feel Like Singing* (Osman and McConochie 1979). This collection of American folksongs contains many valuable teacher aids, but use it with care because of the unusual language and structures it often presents. Read through the eyes of an ESL student, and you'll realize how convoluted the language in "Clementine" is, for example:

> Herring boxes without topses
> Sandals were for Clementine.

This kind of language would obviously confuse a beginning ESL student and could retard progress in conversational English rather than enhance it.

Music has been called the universal language, understood by everyone. Chosen properly, it can provide enjoyment and solid language gains in the ESL classroom.

DRAMA AND ROLE PLAY

Language teaching, like instruction in many areas, often fails to achieve its potential impact because it does not address the whole person. Drama and role play in the classroom combine the intellectual aspects of language, such as vocabulary and structures, with its emotional and practical aspects. Language becomes what it should be—a holistic experience. Drama and role play can also add interest to your classroom while giving your students the opportunity to practice their language skills in realistic situations.

Perhaps the most valuable benefit of drama and role play is that they help remove a major block to English competence: lack of confidence in using the language. Because drama and role play allow students to "step into someone else's shoes," learners are less sensitive about displaying a less-than-perfect command of the language. Once they've taken the plunge, subsequent efforts become easier because their self-esteem increases as they realize they can indeed express themselves adequately in real-world situations.

Skits in English (Hines 1980) provides appropriate dramatic exercises for ESL students at various levels. There's a plus: most of the skits incorporate humor. But the most effective skits for your classroom may be the ones your students create. Have students describe real-life situations in which they need to interact. Depending on the level of the class, you may want to help students develop the skit as a group and prepare the speakers orally in much the same way as you would for a dialogue. A more advanced class might prepare skits in small groups, write them down, verify the language with you, and then perform them for the class. Benefits accrue, then, from many avenues: the motivation of working on situations that are relevant to students; the holistic language experience of understanding, reading, writing, listening, speaking, and acting out situations; the different learning styles accommodated by this approach; and the confidence that arises from devising a means of handling problems.

When introducing drama and role play to your students, be sure to build in success. Ask for volunteers, and coach them as much as necessary before they go "on stage" in front of the class. Allow for practice and feedback in small groups; praise liberally; minimize overt corrections until students feel more at ease. Emphasize the fact that they are playing roles; if they make a mistake, they can blame it on their characters.

One especially beneficial technique for introducing students to role play while teaching important cultural information is the "wrong-way, right-way role play." This technique was developed to a fine art by two Florida adult ESL teachers, Katharine Isbell and Bill Fanning. Isbell and Fanning used the process extensively to develop their higher-level students' interview skills. The design first gives students an opportunity to relax and laugh at some common interview mistakes in a "wrong-way role play." Then students develop interview guidelines, practice their interview skills, and take charge of feedback, which emphasizes the positive while calling attention to areas that need work. This supportive, structured process provides much-needed practice while building self-esteem.

There are seven specific steps in the process. Although the steps listed below use examples based on an interview, many other topics (especially cultural points) can be handled beautifully through the use of the wrong-way, right-way role play.

1. Begin with a wrong-way role play. Have the interviewee (preferably you or someone on staff who is known to the class) do as many things wrong as possible. The more extreme, the better: for example, inappropriate dress for a woman could be illustrated by flashy, dangly jewelry; overly bright or risqué clothing; unkempt hair; spiked, open-backed heels; and too much makeup. Other don'ts that are easy to convey are poor eye contact, lack of interest, failure to find out anything about the company before the interview ("Oh, I thought you manufactured dog food!"), concern *only* with benefits (salary, vacation, sick leave), poor posture (slouching or draping oneself over the chair), discussing personal problems, and so forth. You may even want to illustrate several inappropriate responses with different people so that you can depict a range of behavior from overly shy or indifferent to overly aggressive. This introductory step breaks the ice and relieves tension while helping people recognize some of the things they might need to change. The more exaggerated and outrageous the behavior, the more effective it is because it makes the point while providing humor.

2. Ask the class what was done wrong in the role play. Soliciting their advice and opinions gives students a boost. *They* are telling *you* how to handle a situation instead of you telling them. This confidence-building is expanded in the next step.

3. Have students form small groups and draw up a list of guidelines for the role-play situation. Introduce this step with a comment such as, "You've pointed out what *not* to do. Now I'd like you to list some of the things a person who is being interviewed *should* do." Allow at least ten or fifteen minutes; then have each group share its suggestions with the class as you write them down on a flip chart. Be supportive of the responses, but if a suggestion is inappropriate, don't let it pass. Ask the other group members how they feel about it, or describe a situation to illustrate how it could be detrimental. Present your case as "What if . . . ?" instead of as "Here's why it won't work." Let students tell *you*. If important items have been left off the total list,

ask questions to elicit them. For example, if no one has mentioned arriving on time, ask, "Does it make any difference what time you arrive for the interview?"

These three steps alone provide excellent information for your ESL students. If they want or need further practice, continue with steps 4–7.

4. Help students learn appropriate language for the right-way role play. If you are working on interview skills, you can have students think of specific questions they might be asked in a job interview. They might also work in small groups to develop lists of questions they need to ask an interviewer. Other role-play situations might require other activities, such as choosing appropriate responses. This is also a good time to discuss levels of language. "Catch you later" might be said to a friend, for example, but not to an interviewer.

5. Explain the right-way role play procedure. Announce that students will now practice the *right* way to act in the given situation. Groups of three with rotating duties (two role players and one observer) work well. In the interview situation, for example, one person will act as interviewer, one as interviewee, and one will serve as observer during each rotation. Ask that they make this role play as real as possible. In the interview, for example, they should include the entrance, greeting, and closing. The role players should ask the observer for feedback at the end of each rotation.

6. Talk briefly about giving and receiving feedback. Discuss how people often tend to point out only what is wrong or what needs to be changed when they give feedback. Remind students that we all need to know what we are doing well too! As a general rule, two positive comments should be offered for each recommendation for change.

Point out that (1) receiving feedback can be valuable, (2) this exercise is a learning experience and students are not expected to be perfect, and (3) they can get important information from the feedback that will help them communicate more effectively. The role players should ask directly for feedback, rather than having the observer volunteer comments. This technique gives the individual control over a situation in which he or she is vulnerable.

Feedback questions for the interview situation might include "Did I introduce myself confidently?" "Did I ask the questions I needed to ask?" "Did I sound positive?" After asking several specific questions such as these, the interviewee should ask two summary questions: "If I could change one thing, what should that be?" and "What did I do especially well?" Notice that the feedback questions are designed to build confidence as well as pinpoint weaknesses.

7. Conduct the skill practices. If interviewing is your focus, allow at least ten minutes for each person to be interviewed and at least five

minutes for feedback. Make sure the timetable is followed so that every-one has an opportunity to be the interviewee. Other targeted language situations may require different time frames.

Although this process is suitable only for higher-level students, it can easily be modified for less experienced students by eliminating the steps that require writing. The wrong-way, right-way role play provides a humorous way to approach challenging situations and then develop and practice ways of dealing with them.

For additional information on research relating to the effectiveness of the use of drama in ESL instruction, see Stern's "Why Drama Works: A Psycholinguistic Perspective" (1983).

KINESTHETIC ACTIVITIES

James Asher has based a whole approach to teaching language on the theory that learning can be significantly accelerated through the use of the kinesthetic sensory system—incorporating movement in instruction. Asher refers to his approach as the total physical response system (TPR).

The instructional format of TPR is based on the way we naturally learn language. First is a listening period during which students must follow directions but are not asked to speak, therefore developing understanding before speaking is expected (Asher 1982). The adult beginning to learn a second language through TPR is analogous to the child who cannot speak but can respond to commands such as, "Give it to Mommy," "Look at the cat," "Put that truck in the toy box," and "Point to the bear's nose."

As understanding is demonstrated through movements, students gain confidence in their abilities and are able to give commands of their own. Through use of realia, hand-drawn pictures, and other stimuli in addition to demonstrated commands, students can learn a wide range of vocabulary. Such things as numbers, colors, sizes, and relationships indicated by prepositions are quite easily incorporated into the commands, even at a very early stage. Later, tenses can be incorporated. Throughout the command sequences, humor is used to heighten interest. As an example, here is one of the sentences used in instructing students in Spanish: "When Henry runs to the blackboard and draws a funny picture of Molly, Molly will throw her purse at Henry." (Asher, Kurudo, and de la Torre 1983, p. 65). This zany sentence illustrates a cause-and-effect relationship everyone can understand, creating interest while at the same time teaching the structures of an introductory adverbial clause and the future tense.

Research has continually demonstrated the effectiveness of the TPR approach. Physically responding to commands appears to foster long-term memory with few repetitions. In a study of students learning German by this method, an experimental group with only 32 hours of training had significantly better listening comprehension than college students completing either 75 or 150 hours of college instruction in German. In addition, their skills in reading and writing (in which they had received no training) were comparable with those of a control group that did receive literacy training (Asher, Kurudo, and de la Torre 1983, p. 63).

To understand how exciting this method is for students (and teachers!) and the confidence it builds right from the beginning, simply teach a group of non-English-speakers five verbs: *stand up, sit down, walk, stop,* and *turn.* Illustrate these, and then have students act them out as you command. Next, teach three nouns: *chair, table,* and *window.* Once students have learned a noun in connection with one verb, combine the noun with a different verb. Once you have taught them "Walk to the chair," for example, you can substitute "Walk to the table" or "Walk to the window." Watch as they realize they are responding to a command they have never been taught in a totally new language; the expressions on their faces are the "Aha!" that every teacher seeks to inspire. The effect is hard to imagine unless you experience it or watch others experience it. And the beauty is that this surge of confidence—this "Yes, I can!" feeling—arises in less than ten minutes of instruction.

Asher has developed TPR kits for working with beginning ESL students. Although his concepts can be implemented without the kits, they provide excellent resource material.

Other kinesthetic activities can be worked into a wide variety of lessons. Use a "walking sentence" to introduce a class, for example. You may decide to say, "In class tonight, we will learn about road signs." Print each word in large letters on a separate sheet of paper or large index card. Include a separate card for each punctuation mark. Randomly give each card to a student and ask the recipients to arrange themselves in a sentence. Watch as they discuss the language and proudly arrange themselves in order. As an alternative, the students holding the cards can be directed by the students at their desks. This exercise is not, of course, something that would be effective with beginners early in their instruction, but intermediate classes love it. Once the sentence is unscrambled, place the cards on a window sill, blackboard ledge, or bulletin board so that everyone can see it.

Another kinesthetic exercise based on the same principle is the string sentence. In this case, use clothespins or print the words on large index cards folded in half so that they can be placed over a string. This technique is ideal for teaching or reinforcing the transformation from a statement to a question. It can be done by an individual, or the class can direct the movement of the words and punctuation marks.

Beginners often enjoy a bingo game to review simple words. You hold up a picture, and students cover the word on their cards (or on one large playing card on the blackboard). Antonyms and synonyms also make good bingo games. These games have the added excitement of having a winner with no fault attributed to those who do not win.

As a vocabulary review, you might list several major categories on the board, such as things to eat, things to ride in, and things to wear. Give students cards with names of items in the various categories and have them attach the words in the right place. To review prepositional phrases, ask students to place objects appropriately, for example, "on the floor," "under the table," and "near the door." Add a few unusual ones to heighten interest: "on the teacher's head" or "inside your shoe." Add non-classroom items to extend the benefit of this exercise. If the class is working on reading and writing, the phrases can be written on cards and taped in the appropriate places by students. Depending on student readiness, you might ask each student to write his or her phrase on the board for the class before placing it correctly.

A variation of musical chairs can also provide an enjoyable activity that reinforces language concepts. Instead of having all participants march around until the music stops, call for certain groups: "Everyone who is wearing red change places" or "Everyone who has dark hair . . . ," "Everyone who is married . . . ," "Everyone whose name begins with J . . . ." Obviously, your choices will be based on the level of the class. Again, add interest. When you want all students to move, say, "Everyone who has two feet . . . ," or "Everyone who wants to learn English . . . ."

Several of the activities described above and quite a few others can be found in *A Bag of Tricks for Language Teachers* (Schmelig 1984), an excellent resource for adding interest and excitement while reinforcing important learning skills in the classroom. *Index Card Games for ESL* (English Language Department, The School for International Training 1982) is another good resource, as is *Experiential Language Teaching Techniques* (Jerald and Clark 1983).

With sensory activities, ESL teachers have a unique opportunity to introduce individuals to the English language in a positive, dynamic way. Active involvement of learners in the ESL classroom results not only in more pleasurable learning but in *more* learning. If it works, it's fun, and it's not immoral or illegal, why not do it?

Bibliography

Asher J. 1982. *Learning another language through actions: The complete teacher's guidebook.* 2nd ed. Los Gatos, Calif.: Sky Oaks Productions.

Asher, J., Kurudo, J., and de la Torre, R. 1983. Learning a second language through commands: The second field test. In *Methods that work,* ed. J. Oller and P. Richard-Amato. Rowley, Mass.: Newbury House.

Bancroft, W. 1983. The Lozanov method and its American adaptation. In *Methods that work,* ed. J. Oller and P. Richard-Amato. Rowley, Mass.: Newbury House.

English Language Department, The School for International Training. 1982. *Index card games for ESL.* Brattleboro, Vt.: Pro Lingua.

Graham, C. 1978. *Jazz chants.* New York: Oxford University Press.

———1986. *Small talk.* New York: Oxford University Press.

———1982. *Turn of the century songbook.* New York: Regents.

Guglielmino, L. 1986. The affective edge: Using songs and music in ESL instruction. *Adult Literacy and Basic Education* 10 (1): 19–26.

Hines, M. 1980. *Skits in English.* New York: Regents.

James, W., and Galbraith, M. 1984. Perceptual learning styles: Implications and techniques for the practitioner. *Lifelong Learning* 8(4): 20–23.

Jerald, M., and Clark, R. 1983. *Experiential language teaching techniques.* Brattleboro, Vt.: Pro Lingua.

Kind, U. 1980. *Tune in to English.* New York: Regents.

Larsen–Freeman, D. 1986. *Techniques and principles in language teaching.* New York: Oxford.

Maley, A., and Duff, A. 1978. The use of dramatic techniques in foreign language learning. *Récherches et Échanges* 3.

Oller, J., and Richard-Amato, P., eds. 1983. *Methods that work.* Rowley, Mass.: Newbury House.

Osman, A., and McConochie, J. 1979. *If you feel like singing.* New York: Longman.

Schmelig, F. V. 1984. *A bag of tricks for language teachers.* Self-published: P. O. Box 1863, Palm Harbor, Florida 34273.

Stern, S. 1983. Why drama works: A psycholinguistic perspective. In *Methods that work,* ed. J. Oller and P. Richard-Amato. Rowley, Mass.: Newbury House.

Stevick, E. 1983. Interpreting and adapting Lozanov's philosophy. In *Methods that work,* ed. J. Oller and P. Richard-Amato. Rowley, Mass.: Newbury House.

Williams V. 1983. *Teaching for the two-sided mind.* Englewood Cliffs, N.J.: Prentice-Hall.

9

Preparing ESL Students for the Workplace

Lucy Madsen Guglielmino

MOST ADULTS MUST WORK if they want to eat. In many cases, however, adults with limited English proficiency are unable to find employment. Since one of the most commonly voiced guidelines in modern ESL instruction is "Help them learn language appropriate to their needs," ESL classes that focus on work skills are most appropriate and worthwhile.

While many adults with limited English proficiency cannot find work at all, others are forced to take menial jobs far below their abilities because of their lack of expertise with the language. Performance errors, lack of advancement, and safety problems due to language difficulties often plague them. A number of ESL programs to address the needs of these students are becoming common.

PRE-VOCATIONAL ESL

Many general-purpose ESL classes include one or more units devoted to preparing for the world of work; others are offered specifically as pre-vocational ESL. These classes usually focus on common employment-related skills such as reading and responding to want ads; completing job applications; using appropriate interview techniques, behavior, and language; and completing tax-withholding forms. They may also include language skills such as asking for assistance and verifying instructions. For a sample list of targeted language functions, see the *Vocational English Language Training (VELT) Resource Package,* pages 3–12. Ordering information is given in Chapter 10.

Cultural points related to the job topics covered are (or should be) always included. For example, a discussion of questions and responses that can be used in a job interview will not greatly enhance students' chances of success if they do not understand the cultural points of shaking hands and maintaining eye contact.

Since pre-vocational instruction does not include job-specific vocational language and skills, it can be offered in a regular classroom. Other kinds of vocational ESL are more likely to be offered at a vocational center or on the job site.

OCCUPATION-SPECIFIC VESL IN VOCATIONAL SCHOOLS

Focusing on the language skills required for one specific job, occupation-specific VESL in vocational schools is usually (and ideally) offered in conjunction with the regular vocational instruction. To design the most appropriate instruction, the language instructor should consult with the vocational instructor both initially and continually. The initial consultation should take place long before instruction is scheduled to begin so that there is sufficient lead-time to develop a curriculum focused on the specific vocabulary, grammar structures, and language functions students will need to complete their vocational training successfully. Continuing consultation is necessary for several reasons:

1. To coordinate the timing of your VESL lessons with the presentation of related vocabulary and skills in the vocational class.

2. To obtain realia, pictures, or diagrams needed to prepare students for the vocational instruction or to further explain and reinforce concepts already learned.

3. To verify the impact of your VESL instruction and/or identify problem areas.

4. To identify topics or vocabulary that should be added to your VESL instruction.

Although the primary focus of occupation-specific VESL is on improving language skills needed to perform jobs, basic skills must often be reviewed as well. Students may, for example, need to add or multiply in order to determine correct dimensions, or they may need to know alphabetical order to work with files.

The VELT Resource Package (U.S. Department of Health and Human Services 1985) lists ten factors that contribute to the success of an occupation-specific VELT program:

1. Programs are coordinated with vocational training or direct work experience activities to maximize the chance of success.
2. Sufficient time and resources are allocated for materials development.
3. Occupation-Specific VELT is delivered through a coordinated team effort involving a vocational instructor or worksite supervisor and a vocational English as a second language instructor.
4. For worksite programs, all necessary levels of management are involved to ensure adequate support.
5. Sufficient time and resources are allocated to train instructors.
6. Initial implementation focuses on a small number of occupations, the selection of which is based upon:
    a. local labor market demand
    b. student target population (size, language proficiency, interests, skills, attitudes)
    c. availability of vocational training opportunities
7. The program directly provides or coordinates with the following major components:
    a. recruitment and intake
    b. program orientation
    c. English language and basic skills training
    d. counseling and cultural orientation
    e. job development, job placement, and job follow-up
8. Ongoing needs assessment for program development is implemented to meet the demands of the labor market and the needs of the participants.
9. Supplementary and multiple funding are secured to support initial and ongoing program implementation.
10. Language proficiency requirements for program entrance and exit are based upon:
    a. reasonable expectations of the student population
    b. bona fide communication requirements of vocational training
    c. bona fide communication requirements in the labor market
    (Chapter 3, p. 59)

JOB-SITE ESL

In recent years educators have increasingly taken instruction to the target population rather than waiting for the target population to walk in the door. This trend was fueled by the final report of the Project on Adult Literacy (Chrisman 1989), which strongly stated the need for a greater national focus on "the most seriously neglected national priority" in the field of literacy: basic skills of the work force. The report emphasized the paradox that the vast majority of public and private literacy programs are not available to people on the job, yet increasing the skills of that group offers the greatest potential for short-term economic benefit.

Offering VESL programs in the workplace can result in major benefits to both employee and employer, for the employee receives specific, job-related instruction that reduces communication problems, increases understanding of instructions and procedures, and provides a means of discussing and adapting to cultural differences that otherwise may create problems on the job. Because of the immediate benefits involved, employers are usually willing to assist in a variety of ways. Although practices vary, many employers will not only provide space for class meetings and assistance in scheduling class times, but may also release employees to attend classes and provide a company liaison to give regular feedback to instructors.

Job-site ESL programs originate in a variety of ways. An adult education agency may be asked by representatives of a company to provide ESL instruction on-site. Or the agency may decide to solicit business or industry involvement in such an effort.

As with VESL programs in vocational schools, organizers must allow sufficient time to develop a curriculum that will be relevant and effective. First decide which group(s) of employees to focus on initially and gather specific information about their language needs. To obtain the needed information, you can observe and interview the workers; assess their language levels; examine pertinent printed materials such as manuals, job aids, forms, and signs; and talk with supervisors. Both *English at Work* (Literacy 85, 1985) and *A Handbook of the Job-Site English Project* (Orange County Public Schools 1986) provide checklists to use when interviewing employers. Some curriculum developers even find it necessary to actually work the job for a day or more to ensure that they understand the procedures involved. If the major need is for skills that are common across several jobs, a "cluster VESL" approach, discussed later in this chapter, can be used.

After all the required information is gathered, the next step is to organize the language needs into logical groupings. *English at Work* (Literacy 85, 1985) offers examples of items falling into each of the four general categories of work-specific language needs identified by Jupp and Hodlin (1975):

1. *Job-specific language for job situations,* such as safety warnings, regulations, and basic terms for work processes and materials.
2. *Language for increased job flexibility,* such as answering the telephone when the supervisor is away or training a new employee.
3. *Language for social interaction on the job,* such as greeting co-workers and initiating conversation.

4. *Language for workplace procedures and policies,* such as calling in sick, understanding health benefits, and making insurance claims.

From this point, specific competencies can be defined and reviewed with the employer. Then priorities and the approximate length of time available for instruction will need to be determined.

Once the specific competencies to be covered have been agreed upon, design of the learning plan can begin, including any objectives needed to reach a designated competency and appropriate teaching strategies. Several excellent resources are available to assist in this process. Two— *English at Work* (Literacy 85, 1985) and *A Handbook of the Job-Site English Project* (Orange County Public Schools 1986)—are listed at the end of this chapter.

Feedback

Continual feedback, both from the employer and the students, is essential. Evaluation efforts should focus not only on students' performance in the classroom setting, but also on their job performance. For the program to be effective, the gains must be apparent in the workplace. In addition to in-class testing, then, evaluators might want to devise a brief questionnaire for supervisors, interview class members and supervisors or examine performance figures and error rates. The exact techniques chosen will depend on the specific goals of the evaluation. This constant monitoring may also reveal new needs for learning that can be incorporated into the lessons.

CLUSTER VESL

Probably the newest approach to VESL instruction, cluster VESL refers to grouping students for vocation-related language instruction based on common language needs. Responding to customer requests, asking for clarification, and answering questions, for example, are common to most jobs having a high degree of public contact. A class covering principles and terminology of measurement would be useful for welders, carpenters, and plumbers.

The cluster approach is especially beneficial where there are not sufficient numbers to justify occupation-specific VESL classes, yet more detailed information than a general VESL class can offer is needed. Cluster VESL classes have been offered successfully both in vocational centers and on the job site. Once again, close contact with vocational skills instructors or company representatives is essential for program design, implementation, and evaluation.

The VELT Resource Package is a valuable asset for anyone considering the development of a VESL program. In addition to detailed information on the various approaches described in this chapter, it includes a comprehensive listing of resource programs and persons throughout the United States. Also included are matrices to help you identify specific employment areas (such as clerical, welding, and nurse assistant) and the language background of the population served by each program so that you can quickly locate the most appropriate resources for your own needs. You can read in greater detail about *The VELT Resource Package* in Chapter 10.

Vocational ESL carries tremendous potential for rapidly improving or stabilizing the economic status of adults with limited English proficiency; it also fosters quickly realized economic gains for the companies that employ them. Although these factors make the recent strong emphasis on VESL quite understandable, they should not in any way diminish the importance of more broadly based ESL programs. Individuals with limited English proficiency are not just workers; they need a broad range of language skills to function effectively in all aspects of their lives.

Bibliography

Belfiore, M. E., and Burnaby, B. 1984. *Teaching English in the workplace.* Ontario Institute for Studies in Education.

Chrisman, F. P. 1989. *Jump start: The federal role in adult literacy.* Southport, Conn.: The Southport Institute for Policy Analysis.

Jupp, T. C., and Hodlin, S. 1975. *Industrial English: An example of theory and practice in functional language teaching.* Portsmouth, N.H., Heinemann.

Literacy 85. 1985. *English at work: A descriptive guide to developing an employment-specific ESL curriculum.* Published by author.

Mrowicki, L., et al. 1972. *VESL materials for the job-site.* Northwest Educational Cooperative.

Mrowicki, L., and DeHesus, P. 1981. *Handbook for the VESL teacher.* Northwest Educational Cooperative.

Orange County Public Schools. 1986. *A handbook of the job-site English project, 1985–86.* Published by author.

U.S. Department of Health and Human Services, Social Security Administration, Office of Refugee Resettlement. 1985. *Vocational English language training resource package.*

10

Resources

Lucy Madsen Guglielmino

TAKING ADVANTAGE OF available professional courses, technical assistance, networking possibilities, and program and curriculum guides is vital to being an effective teacher. This chapter compiles some information about such resources for you.

PROFESSIONAL ORGANIZATIONS

Teachers of English to Speakers of Other Languages (TESOL) is an international professional organization of ESL/EFL educators. This organization publishes the *TESOL Quarterly*, *TESOL Newsletter*, and the *TESOL Adult Education Interest Section Newsletter*, all valuable sources of information for keeping up with the field. Its national headquarters are at the following address:

TESOL
1600 Cameron Street
Suite 300
Alexandria, Virginia 22314
(703) 836-0774

Forty-three TESOL affiliates operate within the United States. For the current address of the affiliate in your area, contact the field services coordinator at TESOL's national office. Membership information is also available.

Conferences are sponsored by the international and state TESOL organizations. In some cases, workshops and local training activities are sponsored by state affiliates on a limited basis. Check with your affiliate for details.

For a complete list of other international professional organizations, see "Keeping Up to Date as an ESL Teacher" by Laura Thompson in *Teaching English as a Second or Foreign Language,* edited by Marianne Celce-Murcia and Lois McIntosh (Rowley, Mass: Newbury House, 1979).

PROGRAM STANDARDS AND GUIDELINES

TESOL has developed criteria that adult ESL programs can use in developing an overall plan or in conducting a self-study: *TESOL's Standards for English as a Second Language Programs in Adult Education in English-Speaking Countries.* Experienced professionals in adult ESL throughout the United States contributed to this document, which covers a wide range of topics, including definitions, characteristics of quality adult ESL programs, program administration and operation, instructional design, instructional staff, and program assessment. It provides a good "thought piece" and a reference, both for teachers and administrators. The program standards can be found in the Appendix of this book.

Self-study manuals for four different program categories (including adult education) are also available from TESOL.

CURRICULUM GUIDES

Several available curriculum guides are excellent and valuable resources. A few are described here.

Adult Education Guide to ESL Curriculum

This guide, prepared by the Chicago Urban Skills Institute, presents course content based on communication objectives stated in functional terms (such as giving and seeking information, persuading, and describing). Each objective reflects life situations; appropriate grammar structures and vocabulary are suggested. Levels include ESL Literacy and Beginning, Intermediate, and Pre-Advanced ESL. This guide is available through ERIC (Document #273758).

Adult Refugee ESL Curriculum

Project Work English, a refugee program for adults in Chicago, has developed competency-based curricula for two instructional levels: *Level One: Survival* for beginning students and *Level Two: General Vocational ESL* for high beginning and intermediate students. Each level consists of three tracks—nonliterate, semiliterate, and literate students.

Each level has an introduction explaining the program goals and approach; suggestions for using the curriculum with nonliterate as well as literate students; a list of competencies; instructional units containing situations, sample language forms, brief cultural notes, and textbook resources; special instructional units for the nonliterate student, a list of key competencies for measuring achievement, and performance-based achievement tests. Curricula for both levels are available at cost. Contact:

> Linda Mrowicki, Project Director
> Northwest Educational Cooperative
> 855 Mt. Prospect Road, 2nd floor
> Des Plaines, Illinois 60018
> (708) 803-3535

California Adult Student Assessment System (CASAS)

CASAS is a comprehensive educational assessment system designed to provide a foundation for competency-based curricula for all levels of ABE and ESL instruction for adults. The competency list and curriculum index and matrix essentially provide a curriculum guide. An item bank for initial assessment and for testing achievement of the competencies is available.

CASAS consultants will work with local educators to customize the CASAS resources to meet their needs. Fees are charged to cover consultant time and expenses. Contact:

> California Adult Student Assessment System (CASAS)
> 2725 Congress Street
> Suite 1-M
> San Diego, California 92110
> (619) 298-4681

English as a Second Language Curriculum

Palm Beach County Schools Adult Education has developed detailed curriculum guides for beginning, intermediate, and advanced ESL instruction. They are based on a survival/life skills format organized around ten topics, including personal life, the world of money, food, health, and the law. Appropriate vocabulary and grammar structures are provided for each situation presented. Contact:

Adult ESL Coordinator
Palm Beach County Schools
3323 Belvedere Road
West Palm Beach, Florida 33416-5106

Mainstream English Language Training (MELT) Resource Package

The MELT package was developed over a three-year period by ESL teachers and consultants throughout the United States. It contains a competency-based, outcome-oriented core curriculum guide, a system for defining student performance levels, and a valid and reliable instrument for assessing students' English proficiency—the Basic English Skills Test (BEST)—in three forms to facilitate pre- and posttesting. Administrative manuals for the test are included. MELT was designed as a flexible guide for local program adaptation; it also provides a basis for reliable program comparison, monitoring, and evaluation. This document is available through ERIC (Document #ED264384), as is a separate bibliography (#ED286074).

Vocational English Language Training (VELT) Resource Package

Developed during an intensive yearlong national effort funded by the Office of Refugee Resettlement, the VELT resource package is a goldmine for the teacher. The package was created by a team of expert teachers involved in work-related ESL instruction throughout the United States. It includes steps in planning and implementing a VELT program, descriptions of three types of VELT programs and factors for successful implementation of each type, a list of VELT resource programs and people to contact for more detailed information, and an annotated bibliography of resource materials that are not commercially available, with appropriate contact persons. This package is available through ERIC (Document #ED313536).

CONTACT AND NETWORKING POSSIBILITIES

In addition to TESOL Conferences, many of the state TESOL affiliates will help you get in touch with persons who can answer your questions. Your county or state director of adult education will probably also be able to refer you to ESL contacts.

COLLEGES AND UNIVERSITIES

Many colleges and universities offer courses or even complete programs in ESL and EFL instruction. Their libraries are likely to have good selections of books and other materials on cultural backgrounds and ESL and EFL instruction. Faculty members are usually happy to answer a question or provide a reference on a specific problem as well. To locate the programs in your area, ask your local librarian for the *Directory of Professional Preparation Programs in TESOL in the United States (1986)*, edited by Julia Frank-McNeil. Available from TESOL, this guide describes 196 programs leading to degrees in ESL and includes a survey of state certification requirements.

As you consider your professional preparation and continuing development as an ESL teacher, you might also want to review TESOL'S *Guidelines for the Certification and Preparation of Teachers of English to Speakers of Other Languages in the United States*. These guidelines are reprinted in the Appendix.

RESOURCE CENTERS

Much of the following information on national and local resource centers was compiled by Joyce Fowlkes Campbell, education program specialist of the Division of Adult Education in the U.S. Department of Education.

Adult Education Resource Center

This center provides staff development and technical assistance in ABE, GED, and ESL to local education agencies. An annual publication, *Selected Materials: English as a Second Language Annotated Bibliography*, is available free of charge. Contact:

Adult Education Resource Center
Glassboro State College
307 Girard Road
Glassboro, New Jersey 08028
(609) 863-7131

Center for Applied Linguistics

The Center for Applied Linguistics is a private, nonprofit organization devoted to the study of language and the application of linguistics to cultural, educational, and social concerns. The center publishes books, films, slides, and videotapes for ESL teachers. A series of refugee education guides are available at minimal cost. To request information and/or be placed on the center's mailing list, contact:

Office of Communication & Publications
Center for Applied Linguistics
1118 22nd Street NW
Washington, D.C. 20037
(202) 429-9292

Center for Language Education and Research (CLEAR)

CLEAR carries out research and professional development activities relevant to the education of students with limited English proficiency and those who speak foreign languages. Three major themes for CLEAR are: (1) improving the English proficiency and academic content knowledge of language minority students, (2) strengthening second-language capacities through improved teaching and learning of foreign languages, and (3) improving research and practice in educational programs that meet the needs of language minority and majority students. For more information, contact:

Center for Language Education and Research
University of California–Los Angeles
1100 Glendon Avenue, Suite 1740
Los Angeles, California 90024
(213) 206-1486

Clearinghouse on Adult Education

The Clearinghouse provides referral services, disseminates publications on state and national issues, and acts as an information source for resource materials. Contact:

Clearinghouse on Adult Education
U.S. Department of Education
400 Maryland Avenue, SW
Room 522, Reporters Building
Washington, D.C. 20202-5515
(202) 732-2396

Community and Continuing Education Information Service

This service provides community and continuing education teachers and administrators with professional resources that will help them improve instructional programs in ESL, ABE, and adult secondary education. Some of the services include customized database searches, topical bibliographies, and the CCEIS *Resource Catalog.* Contact:

Community and Continuing Education Information Service
The New York State Education Department
Room 330 E-B
Albany, New York 12234
(518) 474-3636

Dissemination Network for Adult Educators (DNAE)

DNAE identifies exemplary instructional strategies and products relevant to the field of adult education, aids in the dissemination and adoption of these strategies, and identifies and disseminates information regarding copyrighted materials relevant to adult education. A bimonthly publication, *Network News,* is available free of charge. Contact:

Dissemination Network for Adult Educators
1575 Old Bayshore Highway
Burlingame, California 94010
(800) 672-3498 (in California only)
(415) 672-3498
(415) 692-2956

ERIC Clearinghouses

The Educational Resources Information Center (ERIC) has numerous documents on ESL instruction. Two centers are of particular interest to adult ESL teachers.

ERIC Clearinghouse on Language and Linguistics
1118 22nd Street NW
Washington, D.C. 20037
(202) 429-9551

The Clearinghouse on Language and Linguistics prepares a newsletter and bulletin announcing available publications twice a year, in March and September. It is automatically sent to all TESOL members who are U.S. residents. Although the clearinghouse does not maintain an in-house mailing list, it will send recent newsletters and publication lists upon request.

ERIC Clearinghouse on Adult, Career, and Vocational Education
Center for Educational Training for Employment
The Ohio State University
1960 Kenny Road

Columbus, Ohio 43210-1090
(614) 486-3655
(800) 848-4815

This clearinghouse identifies, selects, processes, and disseminates information in education, including adult ESL instruction. Available services include microfiche or paper copies of materials at minimal cost, review and synthesis papers, and computer searches, as well as quite a number of free materials, such as "Guidelines for Working with Adult Learners" and "Strategies for Retaining Adult Students." Upon request, you will receive a newsletter twice a year that lists available publications and services.

Illinois ESL Adult Education Service Center

This center provides a variety of adult ESL staff development activities for teachers and administrators. It also disseminates curriculum and program development materials and provides consultation services. For more information, contact:

Illinois ESL Adult Education Service Center
Northwest Educational Cooperative
1855 Mount Prospect Road
Des Plaines, Illinois 60018
(708) 803-3535

National Clearinghouse for Bilingual Education

This clearinghouse features practitioner-focused services and state-of-the-art technologies to support its information system. Services include a bimonthly newsletter, telephone reference and referral services, occasional papers, program information guides on the education of persons with limited English proficiency, response to requests for information (it maintains a collection of searches on file), and annotated bibliographies on specific issues developed through computerized database searches. Electronic access to its information system is free. Contact:

National Clearinghouse for Bilingual Education
11501 Georgia Avenue
Wheaton, Maryland 20901
(301) 933-9448
(800) 647-0123

PUBLISHERS

Most experienced ESL teachers insist that there is no perfect text; you must supplement and individualize to meet the needs of your students effectively. There is probably no truer statement; however, some excellent texts are now available that can provide a good base from which to build. The publishers listed below produce the most frequently recommended books and materials for ESL instruction, based on a survey of experienced teachers.

Addison-Wesley
Route 128
Reading, Massachusetts 01867

Alemany Press
P. O. Box 5265
San Francisco, California 94101

Bilingual Educational Services
2514 S. Grand Avenue
Los Angeles, California 90007

Cambridge University Press
40 W. 20th Street
New York, New York 10022

David Cook
850 N. Grove Avenue
Elgin, Illinois 60120

Delta Systems
215 N. Arlington Heights Road
Arlington Heights, Illinois 60004

Heinemann Educational Books
70 Court Street
Portsmouth, New Hampshire 03801

Heinle and Heinle
20 Park Plaza
Boston, Massachusetts 02116

Longman, Inc.
95 Church Street
White Plains, New York 10601

McGraw-Hill, Inc.
1220 Avenue of the Americas
New York, New York 10020

Newbury House Publishers, Inc.
10 East 53rd Street
New York, New York 10022

Oxford University Press
200 Madison Avenue
New York, New York 10016

Prentice-Hall Press
Englewood Cliffs,
New Jersey 07632

Regents Publishing Co.
Two Park Avenue
New York, New York 10016

Scott, Foresman and Company
1900 East Lake Avenue
Glenview, Illinois 60025

Sky Oaks Productions, Inc.
P. O. Box 1102
Los Gatos, California 95031

Steck-Vaughn Co.
P. O. Box 26015
Austin, Texas 78755

Publishers of ESL materials often have regional representatives who will work with you to locate appropriate materials for your students. Many of them will also provide examination copies of books you are considering for use and free training sessions for groups of teachers. All of them will be happy to put you on their mailing lists. Specify the level and cultural backgrounds of your students when you write.

PROFESSIONAL READING

You may have heard the old saying that if you're not growing, you're dying. A wide variety of professional books and journals now exists to help you continue to grow as an ESL teacher.

Books

New books are profiled regularly in the *TESOL Adult Education Interest Section Newsletter* and other journals and newsletters in the field. The following "bare-bones bibliography" for ESL teachers was compiled by John F. Haskell of Northeastern Illinois University and appeared in the *TESOL Newsletter* in April 1987. It contains the books mentioned most frequently in the responses of 23 respected ESL teacher trainers.

Stern, H. H. 1983. *Fundamental Concepts of Language Teaching.* Oxford: Oxford University Press. (Mentioned on 12 lists)

Celce-Murcia, Marianne, and Diane Larsen-Freeman. 1983. *The Grammar Book: An ESL/EFL Teacher's Course.* Rowley, Mass.: Newbury House. (On 11 lists)

Richards, Jack, and Theodore Rodgers. 1986. *Approaches and Methods in Language Teaching: A Description and Analysis.* London: Cambridge University Press. (On 9 lists)

Brown, H. Douglas. 1987. *Principles of Language Learning and Teaching.* 2nd ed. Englewood Cliffs, N.J.: Prentice-Hall. (On 9 lists)

Bowen, J. Donald, Harold Madsen, and Ann Hilferty. 1985. *TESOL Techniques and Procedures.* Rowley, Mass.: Newbury House. (On 7 lists)

(Each of the following on six lists):
The *TESOL Newsletter* and the *TESOL Quarterly.*

Stevick, Earl. 1980. *Teaching Languages: A Way and Ways.* Rowley, Mass.: Newbury House.

(Each of the following on five lists):
Blair, Robert. 1982. *Innovative Approaches to Language Teaching.* Rowley, Mass.: Newbury House.

Celce-Murcia, Marianne, and Lois McIntosh. 1979. *Teaching English as a Second or Foreign Language.* Rowley, Mass.: Newbury House.

Krashen, Stephen, and Tracey Terrell. 1983. *The Natural Approach: Language Acquisition in the Classroom.* San Francisco: Alemany Press.

Larsen-Freeman, Diane. 1986. *Techniques and Principles in Language Teaching.* London: Oxford University Press.

McArthur, Tom. 1981. *The Longman Lexicon of Contemporary English.* London: Longman.

Oller, John, and Patricia Richard-Amato. 1983. *Methods That Work: A Smorgasbord of Ideas for Language Teachers.* Rowley, Mass.: Newbury House.

Raimes, Ann. 1983. *Techniques in Teaching Writing.* New York: Oxford Press.

Stevick, Earl. 1976. *Memory, Meaning and Method.* Rowley, Mass.: Newbury House.

Stevick, Earl. 1982. *Teaching and Learning Languages.* London: Cambridge University Press.

Stevick, Earl. 1986. *Images and Options in the Language Classroom.* London: Cambridge University Press.

Journals

Some journals you may find helpful are listed here alphabetically.

English Language Teaching Journal
Oxford University Press
Press Road
Neasden, London NW10
England

English Teaching Forum
Superintendent of Documents
U.S. Government Printing Office
Washington, D.C. 20402-9371

Language Learning
English Language Institute
University of Michigan
2006 North University Building
Ann Arbor, Michigan 48104

Modern English Teacher
Alemany Press
P. O. Box 5265
San Francisco, California 94101

Modern Language Journal
National Federation of Modern Language Teachers Association
Richard B. Shill, Business Manager

Department of Foreign Languages
University of Nebraska
Omaha, Nebraska 68182

Practical English Teaching
Scholastic, Inc.
730 Broadway
New York, New York 10003

TESOL Quarterly
TESOL
1600 Cameron Street
Suite 300
Alexandria, Virginia 22314

Newsletters and Magazines

In addition to the newsletters published by international TESOL, many of the state TESOL affiliates distribute newsletters. Also of interest:

BCEL Newsletter
Business Council for Effective Literacy
1221 Avenue of the Americas
35th Floor
New York, New York 10020

EPIC (English Plus Informational Clearinghouse) *Events*
National Immigration, Refugee and Citizenship Forum
227 Massachusetts Avenue, NE
Suite 120
Washington, D.C. 20002

In America (focuses on working with refugees)
Center for Applied Linguistics
Refugee Service Center
1118 22nd Street, NW
Washington, D.C. 20037

Workplace Literacy
1106 Staghorn Drive, Suite 1000
North Brunswick, New Jersey 08902

SPECIAL ANSWERS FOR SPECIAL NEEDS

This section title is actually the title of a guide to available resources developed with Adult Education Act 310 (now 353) funds. Prepared by the U.S. Department of Education and updated annually, it highlights projects and publications that may be useful in other areas. It is available from the Division of Adult Education, U.S. Department of Education, Washington, D.C. 20202-5515. Sample entries are listed below.

Adult Education ESL Teachers Guide

This manual was developed at Texas A & I University as a survival guide for newly assigned teachers who have had little or no preservice training in teaching ESL and who do not have access to such training. The manual includes a set of beginning-level lessons and intermediate-level lessons accompanied by detailed instructions. It also has a section on teaching the nonliterate adult that includes several lessons for developing basic reading and writing skills. A selected bibliography of ESL materials is included. Available from:

> Mark Walsh
> South Texas Adult Education Center
> Texas A & I University
> Kingsville, Texas 78363
> (512) 595-2861

The cost of $7.50 includes handling and postage. (The guide is also available from ERIC ED No. 260-295.)

Adult ESL Materials List—Illinois, May 1986

Materials for this list were selected based on two criteria: (1) they are frequently used and highly recommended by teachers in the field of adult ESL and (2) they best represent appropriate content and methodology for adult ESL classrooms. General purpose ESL, special purpose ESL, materials for volunteer tutors, and teacher resources are the four major categories in this list. Available from:

> Illinois ESL Adult Education Service Center
> 1855 Mount Prospect Road
> Des Plaines, Illinois 60018

The cost of $4.25 covers reproduction and postage. Make checks payable to CCSD #54.

American Holidays

This guide was developed at the Dona Ana Branch Community College, New Mexico State University, Las Cruces, to teach ESL students about American holidays. Each holiday, its major customs, special ways of celebrating it, and its significance to U.S. history are covered. The units in the guide are divided into two sections: advanced beginning and advanced. Available from:

> The Clearinghouse on Adult Education
> U.S. Department of Education
> Reporters Building, Room 522
> 400 Maryland Avenue, SW
> Washington, D.C. 20202
> (202) 732-2396

There is no cost.

English in the Workplace for Limited English Proficient Adults

This manual, developed by the Fairfax County, Virginia, Public Schools, Office of Adult and Community Education, describes the steps necessary to set up an English-in-the-workplace program for custodial workers. The manual outlines a curriculum; provides reproducible classroom activity sheets, sample lesson plans, flyers, and question-naires; and offers general and specific resources for teachers to use with limited English speakers. Available from:

> Virginia Commonwealth University
> Adult Basic Education Resource Center
> 1015 W. Main Street
> Richmond, Virginia 23284
> (800) 237-0178

There is no cost.

ESL Computer Games and Vocabulary Checklists

This project was developed at Odessa College, Odessa, Texas, to sup-plement a teacher's classroom activities or to be used in an extended language classroom setting. Teacher-made games and vocabulary checklists (Levels 1–3) were adapted from activities in the classroom and made into ESL software. Eight computer disks for use with the Apple II computer were developed with the following games: Con-centration (Levels 1–3), Clothes Bingo (Levels 1–3), Body Bingo (Levels 1–3), Furniture Bingo (Level 3), Tic Tac Toe (Levels 2–3), Password (Levels 2–3), and Parachute (Level 3). Available from:

> Maggie Cunningham
> Director of Adult Education

Schertz-Cibolo University City–ISD
701 Curtis Avenue
Schertz, Texas 78154
(512) 658-5936

The cost is $3.50.

Idea Book for Teachers of English as a Second Language in Adult Basic Education

This idea book, developed at the University of New Mexico, Albuquerque, describes techniques, activities, materials, and placement instruments. Sample needs assessment, ESL placement instruments, lesson plans, and speaking and writing activities are just some of the items included in this book. Available from:

The Clearinghouse on Adult Education
U.S. Department of Education
Reporters Building, Room 522
400 Maryland Avenue, SW
Washington, D.C. 20202
(202) 732-2396

There is no cost.

Integrating ESL and the Workplace

Project staff developed this monograph, which addresses the process of developing ESL materials for entry-level job situations. Included are an annotated bibliography, a sample job description, a sample personal contact form, and a sample performance form. Available from:

Dr. Harold Beder
The Graduate School of Education
Rutgers University
10 Seminary Place
New Brunswick, New Jersey 08903
(201) 932-7531

The cost of reproduction is charged.

Staff Development Guides on English as a Second Language

These training guides and videocassettes were developed by staff members at San Francisco State University to provide background information and guidelines for incorporating the key elements of competency-based adult education (CBAE) processes into beginning and intermediate ESL classrooms. Both guides include information on: (1) modes of instruction, (2) video demonstration, (3) lesson planning and time management, (4) assessment and evaluation, and (5) classroom support services. The emphasis of the videocassettes that accompany the guides is on effective teaching techniques and strategies for organizing instruction in a beginning- or intermediate-level ESL classroom. The guides may be used by one instructor or small groups of instructors on an individualized basis. Available from:

San Francisco State University
Center for Adult Education
1600 Holloway Avenue
San Francisco, California 94132
(415) 338-1083

The cost is $55 for each guide and videocassette (includes the cost of shipping).

OTHER RESOURCES

It is possible that teachers before you have left resources you can use. There may be only a picture file, a list of field-trip sites, or a few professional books; on the other hand, you may find teacher's handbooks or guides of various kinds. Ask! These locally developed resources can be especially helpful if you are new to the area or the system.

A few examples follow:

Teacher Handbook and Curriculum Guide for Use in English as a Second Language Programs

This booklet contains a number of helpful references for the teacher, such as competency lists for ESL/Literacy, ESL/Coping (Survival), and ESL/Pre-Vocational; suggestions for field trips; a lesson plan format sheet; lists of appropriate community agencies; available texts and materials; and a listing of books and pamphlets in the professional library. It was developed for adult education teachers in Broward County, Florida.

An ESL Literacy Resource Guide in Adult Education.

This extensive guide was developed by the Illinois ESL Adult Education Service Center.

Handbook to Start Beginners in ESL

This photocopied, consumable packet of materials for nonliterate beginners is designed to help them develop a personal information card (name, address, telephone, Social Security number, age, birthdate), learn the alphabet and numbers, and practice writing in manuscript and cursive. It was developed by Orange County Schools (Florida) ESL teachers.

If resources such as these are unavailable in your area, you may want to begin compiling those you think would be most helpful.

CHAPTER

11

A Short Set of Guidelines for Effective ESL Teaching

Lucy Madsen Guglielmino

IF YOU ARE a new ESL teacher, one of the best ways to succeed in your new position is to find persons who do it well, watch them, and ask questions. This short chapter provides another way to do just that. A group of highly successful ESL teachers and supervisors were asked what tips they would give. Their responses follow. Some have been discussed in this book; all represent a combined total of several hundred years' experience of ESL teaching.

If you are an experienced ESL teacher, you know that one of the best ways to grow and improve in your field is to meet and compare notes with your peers. This set of guidelines gives you the opportunity to attend such a "conference." You will probably have tips of your own to add.

The first day of class—

1. Learn the students' names and how to pronounce them. Use nametags to help students learn each other's names as well.

2. Find out something about your students' backgrounds if possible. This information would include native country, first language, level of education, job experience, and length of time in this country.

3. Create a comfortable, nonthreatening atmosphere.

4. Find out students' needs in the four skill areas: listening, speaking, reading, and writing. This does not mean you must administer a formal test on the first day.

5. Determine some short-term goals.

6. Set up a clear system of signals so that students know when you want them to repeat what you have said.

Then and thereafter—

1. Speak in a natural tone of voice. Use normal intonation, rhythm, pace, and volume.

2. Teach by topic, situation, or competency (in other words, teach for a purpose).

3. Make sure your subject matter is relevant. Your students should leave class every day with language they can use.

4. Limit your language in quantity and complexity.

5. Proceed slowly. Don't feel pressured to run through a text.

6. Remember: There is no perfect text. Adapt, adjust, and add to meet your students' needs.

7. Allow adequate time for practice of new vocabulary and language structures. The amount of drill and repetition needed can be surprising.

8. Review every day.

9. Vary activities frequently.

10. Don't correct every error when students begin to speak.

11. Avoid totally negative feedback when an error is made.

12. Help students set small, incremental goals.

13. Give students a chance to learn on their own. Don't teach everything.

14. Care about your students' lives, and show it.

15. Be flexible. The best language lesson may grow from a student's shared experience (an accident, a wedding, anything that is important to students).

16. Start learning a foreign language yourself, to see how difficult it is.

17. Don't be threatened by what you don't know. As Winston Churchill once said, "It is better to do something than to do nothing while waiting to do everything." There is an array of approaches, methods, and materials in ESL instruction. This reservoir of possibilities sometimes intimidates teachers, but if you are committed to helping your students learn English (and you are, or you wouldn't be reading this guide), you will develop an approach that works well for you and your students.

About the Authors

Jeffrey P. Bright has worked in adult ESL as a teacher, teacher trainer, consultant, curriculum writer, and administrator. He is director of literacy programs for the Albany Park Community Center in Chicago. He has written teacher training manuals and scripts for videotapes and co-authored a major curriculum guide and accompanying student text for City Colleges of Chicago.

Lucy M. Guglielmino holds a doctoral degree in adult education and teaches in the graduate program at Florida Atlantic University in Boca Raton, Florida. She has extensive experience in the design and delivery of professional development programs for adult educators. This book grew out of a two-year statewide staff development program she created for adult ESL teachers in Florida. She has served on the governing board of her state TESOL organization and on advisory boards for numerous special projects in ESL, including a Ford Foundation project to develop a model workplace-literacy program in Miami.

John Haskell is a professor of linguistics and TESL at Northeastern Illinois University in Chicago. He has been an ESL teacher of children and adults and a teacher trainer in Michigan, New York, California, Hawaii, and Illinois as well as Japan, Micronesia, Puerto Rico, and Canada. He is past president of TESOL and past editor of the TESOL Newsletter.

Barbara A. Humak is director of human resources for a New Jersey manufacturer that employs large numbers of non-native speakers. She formerly served as ESL resource teacher for the Broward County Schools Adult Education Program in Fort Lauderdale, Florida. She has taught ESL at all levels and has conducted numerous teacher training workshops.

Jerry L. Messec of Florida State University is currently a research associate for Improving the Efficiency of Educational Systems (IEES), a project funded by the Agency for International Development to prepare educational plans for developing countries. He also does extensive ESL and EFL consulting and training within the United States. He has authored twelve textbooks in adult and community education and is senior editor of a multivolume textbook series in academic ESL.

F. Anne Mock served for ten years as adult ESL coordinator for the Palm Beach County Schools, following eighteen years of teaching EFL in Colombia, South America. She recently directed a project to prepare a three-level competency-based ESL curriculum.

Faye Van Arsdall Schmelig, after many years of teaching and supervising adult ESL classes, is now working as a private ESL consultant and teacher trainer. She wrote *English: Your Second Language,* an ESL textbook series, and *A Bag of Tricks for Language Teachers.*

Dr. Julia Spinthourakis is the ESL consultant for the Florida Department of Education. She has thirteen years of experience in research and teaching ESL, both in the United States and Greece. Her doctoral research was in the area of language assessment and testing.

Statement of Core Standards for Language and Professional Preparation Programs

TESOL

INTRODUCTION

This document contains a draft of the TESOL standards for programs designed to teach English to Speakers of Other Languages (ESOL) and for programs designed to prepare professionals for teaching in the field.

The standards presented here are meant to serve as part of an ongoing process of self-study to be conducted by the staff of a program with the support and assistance of the TESOL organization.[1]

---

[1] At its mid-year meeting in October, 1984, the Executive Board reaffirmed its commitment to these standards and the program for self-evaluation. TESOL encourages program staffs to initiate self-regulation through self-study.

Programs which endorse these standards will be invited to send a letter to the TESOL Central Office stating the endorsement. The next step in the process will be conducting a self-evaluation. The results of the self-evaluation including documentation will then be filed with the TESOL Central Office. Having a letter on file which endorses the standards is prerequisite to filing the report on the program self-evaluation. Programs which file endorsements and documented reports of self-evaluations will be recognized. The greatest effectiveness of the self-study approach, however, comes from the dynamic interaction of the review process as it evolves among and with the staff and administration.

STATEMENT OF CORE STANDARDS FOR LANGUAGE AND PROFESSIONAL PREPARATION PROGRAMS

This past half century has seen a rapid and significant rise in the use of English throughout the world. The number of programs providing English language training for speakers of other languages and the number of programs offering degrees and training in the teaching of English to speakers of other languages have increased accordingly.

Teaching English to speakers of other languages is an academic field requiring special programs for its students and special professional education and preparation for its practitioners. Although the name of the organization is Teachers of English to Speakers of Other Languages, its members include researchers and administrators, materials developers and testing specialists, classroom teachers and linguists, as well as specialists in the area of teaching standard English as a second dialect. As the largest professional association dedicated to teaching English to speakers of other languages, TESOL proposes the following set of standards for quality programs to improve ESOL instruction and preparation of professionals in the field.

I. LANGUAGE TEACHING PROGRAMS
Programs for teaching English to Speakers of Other Languages (ESOL programs) with many students or with only a few adhere to basic principles and goals. Presented here are statements of standards that the TESOL organization believes to be inherent in quality programs.

A. STATEMENT OF PURPOSE AND GOALS
A quality program of teaching English to speakers of other languages is based upon a set of principles which recognize that all associated with the program—instructional and support staffs, administrators and students—have a wide range of needs and the

basic right to pursue the fulfillment of those needs; that language is an essential tool for communication and the fulfillment of academic and personal needs; that there are differences between first and second language learning; and that all languages and cultures are worthy of respect and appreciation.

A quality program establishes goals which are based on these principles and which guide the program in the development, implementation and evaluation of appropriate performance objectives and operational procedures. These goals are readily available in a written statement which describes the purpose, scope and nature of the program.

B. PROGRAM STRUCTURE

1. Administration

A quality program of English to speakers of other languages is under the direction of a professionally-educated administration which is knowledgeable and supportive of the program goals and objectives. The administration implements the principles of mutual responsibility and participatory management in personnel practices, utilization of resources, supervision of program staff and evaluation of program activities. Throughout the decision-making process, input from the instructional staff, support staff and students is sought and utilized in an atmosphere of trust and respect.

2. Instructional Staff

A quality program employs instructional staff who have professional preparation and experience for the duties assigned them. Permanent, full-time positions are created and maintained to the fullest extent possible with the role of each member of the instructional staff clearly defined in terms of the total program and the larger institution. Scholarly and professional development, such as research and publication and/or participation in workshops, study groups, professional organizations and coursework is encouraged and supported by the institution and program administration. Opportunities for advancement, essential to the best performance of the instructional staff, are provided. All instructional staff members are treated equitably and compensated comparably within the program and within the larger institution.

3. Support Services

A quality program recognizes that students with limited English proficiency need special attention and provides adequate support services to both students and instructional staff. Examples of support services for students include counseling, classroom space and extra-curricular activities; for instructional staff, quality materials, office space and secretarial support.

C. PROGRAM CURRICULUM

A quality program of teaching English to speakers of other languages implements a curriculum that indicates expected learner outcomes in the various instructional components. Methods and materials, selected and/or developed for the particular age, skill level and needs of the students, are compatible with the goals of the program. Instructional decisions, such as format and intensity of the program, class size, program and course objectives, learning activities and performance standards are made to serve the needs and interests of the student, the institution and society at large. The administrative and instructional staff share in the responsibility for this decision-making with systematic input from the students served by the program.

D. PROGRAM IMPLEMENTATION

A quality program of English to speakers of other languages is implemented in a systematic manner following the progression of assessment, instruction, evaluation, review and revision. Upon entry into the program, students are fairly and appropriately assessed with these results dictating the instructional placement, approach and materials for each student. Accurate records are kept on each student and the instructional program is coordinated with other services which the student may be receiving. Progress is measured at regular intervals to determine growth or changes in student performance.

A quality program provides the public with clear and honest information regarding its purposes, nature and goals as well as information about the community in which the program is located. The cultural, personal, and/or career needs of students, as well as the preferences of sponsors, parents, or guardians, are recognized and respected.

E. PROGRAM ASSESSMENT

A quality program of teaching English to speakers of other languages periodically reviews its objectives, resources and operation in order to determine the program's strengths and weaknesses. Curriculum content, materials and methodologies are scrutinized in relation to student achievement and goals. Availability, cost and quality of human and material resources are considered in program review. Periodic student assessment throughout the program operation and in follow-up studies assures awareness of changing needs and facilitates adjustment of various program decisions such as student placement and scheduling, staff assignments, instructional strategies and extracurricular considerations.

A quality program evaluates its effectiveness on a continual basis as determined by the program staff, administration and students, as well as when required by outside agencies or the larger institution in which the program operates.

II. PROFESSIONAL PREPARATION PROGRAMS

Although the organizational structure of professional preparation programs may differ in various institutions, the principles and goals adhered to throughout the varied professional preparation programs remain the same. Presented here are statements of standards the TESOL organization believes to be inherent in quality programs of professional preparation.

A. STATEMENT OF PURPOSE AND GOALS

A quality program of professional preparation for teaching English to speakers of other languages is based on the same principles as the English language teaching programs. Additionally, since such a professional preparation program is usually offered in an institution of higher education, its goals and purposes must be consistent with those of the institution under which it functions.

A quality program establishes goals which are based on these principles and which guide the program in the development, implementation, and evaluation of performance objectives (competencies) and operational procedures. Since the professional preparation program prepares teachers for many kinds and levels of programs, it may have a number of orientations reflected in its goals. These goals are readily available in a written statement which describes the purpose, scope and nature of the program.

B. PROGRAM STRUCTURE

1. Administration

A quality program of ESOL professional preparation is a designated unit of an institution of higher education. This unit is under the direction of faculty members, knowledgeable and supportive of the program goals and objectives, who have the major responsibility for organizing and coordinating the activities of the program. The faculty, support staff and students are systematically involved in the decision-making process regarding personnel practices, utilization of resources, supervision of program staff and evaluation of program activities.

2. Instructional Staff

A quality ESOL professional preparation program employs faculty who have scholarly preparation and professional experience for the duties assigned them. Permanent, full-time positions are created and maintained to the fullest extent possible with the role of each faculty member clearly defined in terms of the total program. All faculty are treated equitably and compensated comparably within the program and within the larger institution. The administration of the institution of higher education encourages the faculty to engage in scholarly activities, exploration of teaching and service, thereby enriching the program and the field.

3. Support Staff

A quality ESOL professional preparation program provides a trained support staff which includes secretaries, advisors, librarians and, perhaps, technologists.

C. PROGRAM CURRICULUM

It is recognized that there is a great deal of variation in the goals and objectives of professional preparation programs in teaching English to speakers of other languages. However, regardless of the variation, each program should have courses which present basic theory and practice covering the second language and teaching paradigm, such as those guidelines TESOL and other professional organizations have established.[2]

D. PROGRAM IMPLEMENTATION

A quality ESOL professional preparation program ensures that quality instruction is available to all students on all levels; that its courses are appropriate and relevant to the needs of its students; and that its requirements for graduation are clearly written and available to students when they enter the program. Instructional staff and administration attend to record keeping, orientation and assessment of needs throughout the time the student is in the program and in follow-up studies.

---

[2] Refer to the TESOL publication Guidelines for the Certification and Preparation of Teachers of English to Speakers of Other Languages in the United States.

E. PROGRAM ASSESSMENT

A quality program of professional preparation for teachers of English to speakers of other languages systematically and periodically reviews its goals, objectives, resources and operations to determine its strengths and weaknesses. The needs of its students, trends in the field, and the course offerings and their content are scrutinized in relation to student achievement and goals. Periodic assessment and/or counseling throughout the program operation and in follow-up studies assures awareness of changing needs and facilitates adjustment of various program decisions.

In a quality program, evaluation of effectiveness is undertaken as determined by the program staff, administration and students, as well as when required by outside agencies or the larger institution in which the program operates.

Prepared by the Committee on Professional Standards, Carol J. Kreidler, Chairperson. This statement of core standards is the culmination of work begun in December 1982.

Guidelines for the Certification and Preparation of Teachers of English to Speakers of Other Languages in the United States

TESOL

THIS STATEMENT, DESIGNED *primarily to apply to teachers of English to speakers of other languages in the United States of America, will assist teacher certification agencies and educational institutions in the establishment of certification standards for English-as-a-second-language teachers, and in the design and evaluation of ESL teacher education programs. The statement: (A) defines the role of the ESL teacher in American schools, (B) describes his personal qualities and professional competencies, and (C) states the objectives and characterizes important features of a teacher education program designed to develop ESL teachers of high professional ability.*

FOREWORD

Teaching English as a second language has been an educational activity in this country for more than three hundred years. Only in the last twenty-five has it become a profession, making systematic application of a collected body of knowledge combined with learning theory. Its importance has been heightened by the critical role of the English language in the nation's educational process and by the unfortunate circumstance that ethnic and racial minorities have not always been well served by classroom practices designed for native speakers of English.

The teacher of English as a second language has a difficult task. He must set the goals of achievement for his pupils higher than those of his colleagues in the modern foreign languages, yet he must adopt certain of their practices. For those whom he teaches, a working command of English is an educational essential, but this command must be acquired through methods which differ from those customarily employed by the teacher of English to native speakers of the language. In essence this constitutes the case for a special pattern of preparation for teachers of English as a second language.

We recognize that because of the great variation in educational institutions which prepare, or should prepare, such teachers, it is scarcely to the point to work out a set curriculum or to recommend a series of course titles. It is not only useful but urgent, however, to formulate the principles upon which such a program of teacher preparation should rest, especially at a time when education throughout the country must be diversified in a way which will recognize the existence of multilingual and multicultural behavior and when the English language must be viewed as a means of enabling the individual to participate in ever-widening social groups.

Accordingly we have set forth the principles which follow in the form of general guidelines which emphasize personal qualities, attitudes, skills, experience, and knowledge rather than courses and credit hours. The manner of the formulation owes much to the documents entitled *Guidelines for the Preparation of Teachers of English* and *Guidelines for Teacher Education in Modern Foreign Languages*, and like them, represents the consensus of a number of leaders in the field, drawn from all levels of instruction and supervision, representing a broad range of experience and points of view.

Despite the fact that these guidelines are intended to be applicable to teachers at any level, one cardinal principle has been rigidly observed throughout, namely that the teacher of English as a second language should have the same general academic preparation as teachers of other subjects at comparable levels.

Although there are these elements in their preparation which teachers of English as a second language share with others, the uniqueness of their educational responsibility must not be overlooked, nor should we forget that the guidelines set forth here are designed to prepare teachers for this particular task. They are not guidelines for teachers of English in general. Nor do they fully cover for teachers of Standard English as a second dialect or for teachers in bilingual schools, although clearly they would have many elements in common with the preparation of such teachers. In their present form they represent the best effort of which the authors were capable, to develop the outlines of a program both humanely and scientifically oriented toward the achievement of a highly specific but nevertheless a socially critical educational goal.

QUALIFICATIONS AND GUIDELINES

The Preparation of the American School Teacher. These guidelines are intended to suggest desirable competencies for the teacher of English to speakers of other languages. In common with that of all teachers, his preparation will be based on a sound general education—courses and experiences which help him become a well- educated person with a strong background in the liberal arts and sciences, including psychology. *Academic specialization* courses and experiences help him to become proficient in the area of concentration; and *professional education* courses and experiences help him prepare himself as a teacher.

The statement which follows presupposes concurrent or prior completion of the baccalaureate degree program and is therefore concerned primarily with academic specialization and professional education. Its purposes are: (A) to define broadly the role of the English-as-a-second-language teacher in American schools, (B) to describe his personal qualities and professional competencies, and (C) to state the minimal objectives for a teacher education program designed to develop professional competencies and to characterize the features of such a program.

A. THE ROLE OF THE ENGLISH-AS-A-SECOND-LANGUAGE TEACHER IN AMERICAN SCHOOLS

The teacher of English to speakers of other languages in American schools is expected to:

1. Progressively develop in his students comprehension of and ability to interact with English-speaking American society through mastery of communicative competence in English as it is used by the English-speaking population.

> Help his students gain mastery of both receptive (listening and reading) and productive (speaking and writing) English-language skills.

Help his students gain an awareness of and respect for similarities and differences between the English-speaking culture and their own cultural heritage.

Help his students gain knowledge of American social customs, traditions, folklore, history and literature in such a way as to contribute to their mastery of the language and culture, and their future educational and social development.

2. Evaluate his students' progress toward the above objectives, identify their strengths and weaknesses in performance, and adjust their instruction appropriately.

3. Make judicious selection and use of approaches, methods, techniques, procedures, materials and aids appropriate to effective language teaching for his pupils and curriculum objectives.

Evaluate the effectiveness of these teaching procedures and materials in bringing about student behaviors appropriate to the curriculum objectives, and revise their use as necessary.

Maintain vitality in the instructional program by implementing changes in the goals, procedures and materials whenever such changes are indicated by changes in the teaching situation, or by developments in language-teaching theory and practice.

4. Correlate the sequence and scope of his teaching with that in other instructional areas in the curriculum; and contribute to the definition of curriculum goals for linguistic minority students in English-as-a-second-language specifically, and in other areas generally.

B.   PERSONAL QUALITIES, PROFESSIONAL COMPETENCIES AND EXPERIENCE OF THE ENGLISH-AS-A-SECOND-LANGUAGE TEACHER IN AMERICAN SCHOOLS

To achieve the objectives of his teaching role the teacher of English as a second language in American schools is expected to:

1. Have personal qualities which contribute to his success as a classroom teacher, ensure understanding and respect for his students and their cultural setting, and make him a perceptive and involved member of his community.

2. Demonstrate proficiency in spoken and written English at a level commensurate with his role as a language model. Whether he is a native-language or second-language speaker of English,

his command of the language should combine qualities of accuracy and fluency; his experience of it should include a wide acquaintance with writings in it.

3. Have had the experience of learning another language and acquiring a knowledge of its structure; and have a conscious perception of another cultural system. If possible, the language and cultural system should be related to that of the population with which he is to work.

4. Understand the nature of language; the fact of language varieties—social, regional, and functional; the structure and development of the English language systems; and the culture of English-speaking people.

5. Have a knowledge of the process of language acquisition as it concerns first and subsequent language learning and as it varies at different age levels; and understand the effects on language learning of socio-cultural variables in the instructional situation.

6. Have an understanding of the principles of language pedagogy and the demonstrated ability, gained by actual teaching experience, to apply these principles as needed to various classroom situations and instructional materials.

7. Have an understanding of the principles, and ability to apply the techniques and interpret the results of second-language assessment of student progress and proficiency; and ability to evaluate the effectiveness of teaching materials, procedures, and curricula.

8. Have sophisticated understanding of the factors which contribute to the life styles of various peoples, and which determine both their uniqueness and their interrelationships in a pluralistic society.

C. OBJECTIVES AND FEATURES OF A TEACHER EDUCATION PROGRAM IN TEACHING ENGLISH AS A SECOND LANGUAGE

A program to prepare a beginning English-as-a-second-language teacher must provide him with the opportunity to develop the academic and professional competencies set forth in Section B above. These competencies will be developed to a level of proven ability capable of enabling him to fulfill satisfactorily the role-objectives specified in Section A above, as demonstrated through actual teaching responsibility under experienced supervision.

The program features instruction and experiences which contribute directly to development of competencies in linguistics and English linguistics, psycholinguistics, language pedagogy and assessment, including supervised teaching experience and studies in culture. In addition, the program requires objective assessment of both the English and foreign-language proficiency of all candidates, and provides or arranges for supplementary instruction whenever necessary.

A teacher education program may be viewed as having five main components with overlapping competency objectives. The list of topics and experiences given here (with cross references to Section B above) is not intended to be exhaustive or limiting, but only broadly suggestive of the content of each instructional component.

1. *Academic specialization.* Courses and training with the primary objective of helping the student to understanding and knowledge of the nature of language, English-language systems, language learning, and language in culture.

a. Linguistics and English linguistics (B4) – the nature of language, its systematic organization, variation and change; major models of linguistic description; major subsystems of present-day English (grammatical, phonological/graphemic and lexical/semantic), its historical development and dialectical variation; contrastive linguistics with special reference to the comparison of English and a "linguistic minority" language.

b. Psycholinguistics and sociolinguistics (B5) – language acquisition processes in first and second language learning, age differentials in language learning, individual learning styles; basic socio-cultural variables in language use and language learning, types of bilingual and multilingual educational situations, social determiners of dialect and style.

c. Culture and society (B3, B4, B5, B8) – the elements of sociocultural systems; cultural pluralism in American society; description, comparison and interrelationship of English-speaking and linguistic-minority cultures; culturally determined life styles and learning styles and their effect on second language learning.

2. *Pedagogy.* Foundations, methods, and practicum – courses and training with the primary objective of providing theoretical and methodological foundations and practical experience leading to competence in actual teaching situations.

a. Professional education – social foundations and organization of American education, human growth and development, learning theory and curriculum development, including the place of English as a second language in the curriculum.

b. Second-language pedagogy (B6) – objectives, theoretical approaches to, and methods of teaching English as a second language; language-teaching techniques and procedures; curricula, teaching materials and aids; adaptation of instructional materials to specific situations; professional information sources: journals, research reports, and professional organizations; design, implementation and evaluation of innovative materials and techniques.

c. Second-language assessment (B7)—principles of testing; techniques and interpretation of second-language assessment of student progress and proficiency; evaluation of teaching materials, procedures, and curricula.

d. Language teaching practicum (B6, B7)—systematic directed observation, supervised teaching practice, and progressive teaching responsibilities which contribute to experience and competence in the primary roles of the English-as-a-second-language teaching described in Section A above. (Although experience gained in the training program will usually be more extensive and direct in the roles that help shape student behaviors (A1-A2) than in those roles more broadly concerned with curriculum development and evaluation (A3-A4), opportunities should be made available for some experience in all roles.)

(1) The institution provides opportunities for systematic, directed observation of a variety of English-as-a-second-language teaching situations for children, adolescents, and adults at beginning, intermediate, and advanced levels of instruction, and which employ a representative variety of appropriate teaching methods, materials, and aids.

(2) The institution provides directed teaching practice with progressively increasing responsibility, under expert supervision in teaching situations appropriate to the student teacher's employment goals. Through this experience the candidate will both develop and demonstrate his actual and potential ability as an English-as-a-second-language teacher by achieving at least a "good" level of competence in the role-objectives of Section A above.

3. *Another language.* Learning experience, structural and cultural information (B). For those candidates who have not had recent experience learning another language, the institution offers, or provides by special arrangement, second-language instruction. Whenever possible, courses are available by which the candidate can gain knowledge of the linguistic structure of the language and features of the cultural system of the population with which he intends to work.

4. *Evaluation of candidates.* Evaluation of each candidate's achievement in the areas of competence outlined above is an integral and systematic part of the teacher education program at all its stages (i.e., for admission to, retention in, and completion of the program).

a. English language proficiency (B2) of both native and nonnative speakers is demonstrated by satisfactory completion of appropriate college-level course work requiring a high level of oral and written expression and/or objective assessment by standardized test instruments properly interpreted.

b. The institution publishes a clearly formulated policy concerning admission to, retention in, and successful completion of the teacher education program. The statement of this policy includes precise information about application procedures and criteria for admission to the program; it indicates how and by what professional criteria students may be eliminated from the program; and it sets forth clearly the minimal academic achievement and level of teaching competence required for successful completion of the program.

c. The institution evaluates the candidate's achievement by instruments appropriate to the measurement of each competency, including direct evaluation of teaching performance. The results of the evaluation are available for advising the candidate in his continuing education and career development, and for recommending, licensing, and employing him. His readiness to teach is certified in the name of the whole institution. An official designated to make such certification is able to demonstrate that he has received assessments concerning the candidate's performance in all units of the teacher education program.

5. *Staff and facilities.* The institution has a staff whose combined competencies are superior to the level of instructional proficiencies which are the objectives of the program. The teachers and supervisors of courses and training in teaching methodology are themselves superior in the competencies outlined in Section B above.

The institution maintains an up-to-date curriculum materials collection comprising materials, aids, and equipment commonly used in teaching English as a second language at all levels. Journals, research reports, and other sources of supportive professional information are available and kept current.

The institution maintains close contact with the instructional programs in which candidates serve their observation and directed teaching practice assignments.

Revised by William E. Norris based on criteria adopted by the TESOL Guidelines Conference, May 29–30, 1970, and a preliminary draft by James E. Alatis. Foreword by Albert H. Marckwardt.

These guidelines were distributed to the profession, discussed at the TESOL Convention in Washington in 1972 as well as at other conventions and among the TESOL regional affiliates, and ratified by the Executive Committee of TESOL on March 7, 1975, in Los Angeles.